Treasures of the Taylorian:
Series Two: Writers in Residence
Volume 5

Luisa Hewitt

The Girl Who Lived in the Library

Edited by Christina Ostermann

Series Editor: Henrike Lähnemann

Taylor Institution Library, Oxford, 2025

Typesetting by Henrike Lähnemann
Cover design by Emma Huber
Cover image based on a photograph of the Taylor Institution before the extension of 1932. c1880s,
Oxford, Bodleian Libraries, University Archives, TL 5/11

ISBN 978-1-0686058-5-7

Printed in the United Kingdom and United States
by Lightning Source for Taylor Institution Library

Table of Contents

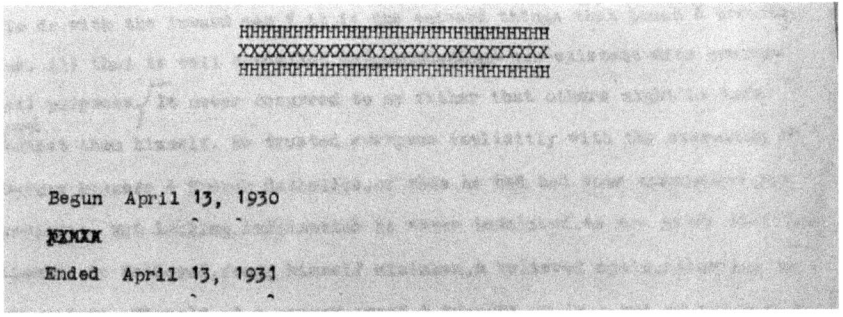

MS. Top. Oxon. d. 440, p. 336, last page of chapter 36 by Luisa Hewitt

Previous volumes in 'Treasures of the Taylorian'
Open access available at https://editions.mml.ox.ac.uk/publications/

Preface

The library and its holdings have been at the heart of all publications of the 'Treasures of the Taylorian' with series covering the Reformation Pamphlets of the Institute (series one), exhibitions and related explorations into the cultural history of literature (series three), and the current series 'Writers in Residence', but never before has a title been so literally true as in this case. Luisa Hewitt grew up in the Taylorian and describes the working of the library and the whole university set-up interlinked with it from an insider perspective.

It is particularly gratifying to have a female author contributing her views on an institution which only late and hesitatingly granted access to women. This fits in very well with the previous volumes in the series which all feature female writers and have a clear thread of feminist writing running through it. The series started with Ulrike Draesner's 'radical translation' of seventeen Shakespeare sonnets and continued with the Japanese-German author Yoko Tawada and the exhibition 'Von der Muttersprache zur Sprachmutter'.

Volumes 3 and 4 link even more closely to Luisa Hewitt's novel since they are both creative responses to German literature and the Modern Languages teaching here in Oxford, no. 3 an anthology of text and images as homage to E.T.A. Hoffmann by a finalist student based on her experiences during her Year Abroad in Bamberg, and no. 4 a collective, feminist translation of a Hedwig Dohm novella by four second-year students and their translation tutor Marie Martine.

My gratitude is to Modern Languages alumna Christina Ostermann who not only edited this volume but also helped curate the linked exhibition 'German in the World' for the 2025 conference of the 'Association of German Studies' (published as volume 8 of the series 'Cultural Memory' of the Taylor Editions) and to the librarians of the Taylorian who magnificently came together for a treasure-hunt through the library to identify locations mentioned, sourced images, cleared copyright, and proof-read the volume.

Last but not least the thanks go to Luisa Hewitt who left her manuscript to the Taylorian with a well-formulated donation letter to allow us to dive with her into the history of the building and also a fascinating chapter of intellectual history of Modern Languages in Oxford.

Henrike Lähnemann
Oxford, August 2025

The 'Institutio Tayloriana' seen from St Giles in 2022.
Photograph Henrike Lähnemann

The Girl Who Lived in the Library
Editor's Introduction
CHRISTINA OSTERMANN

Luisa Hewitt's *roman à clef* and autobiography, *The Chronicle of Wisa Dingeldey by Herself*, offers a vivid account of life at the Taylor Institution Library at the end of the 19th century.[1] As the only child of Heinrich Krebs, Librarian of the Taylorian from 1871 to 1921, Luisa spent much of her childhood living with her father in the basement of the Institution, gaining first-hand insight into its early years, its workings, and its personnel.

In her early fifties, Hewitt looked back and reconstructed her childhood memories from the age of four to the age of 17, that is from around 1885 to 1897/98.[2] She did so over the course of a year, from 13 April 1930 to 13 April 1931.[3] Her memoirs were meant to be her first novel, after she had already published a number of poems.[4] She

---

[1] The building of the Taylor Institution was completed in 1844. The first regulations of the Taylor Institution Library were passed a year later, and the statute was finalised in 1847. The library officially opened in 1849, see the historical overview by Jill Hughes, former German Subject Librarian at the Taylorian, published in: Bernhard Fabian (ed.), *Handbuch der historischen Buchbestände in Deutschland*. Hildesheim: Olms Neue Medien, 2003; accessible online via the Fabian database at the University of Göttingen. Charles H. Firth, *Modern Languages at Oxford, 1724–1929*. London: Oxford University Press, H. Milford, 1929. Christina Ostermann, German(s) at Oxford. The Taylorian in the 19th Century, in: *German in the World. Exhibition Catalogue for the Association for German Studies Conference 2025*. Ed. by Henrike Lähnemann and Christina Ostermann, 2025, pp. 1–14.

[2] Hewitt's year of birth is not recorded, but her autobiography offers clues: annotations to chapter 3, 'My Earliest Memory' (not included in this partial edition), suggest that she was four years old in 1885. This places her birth around 1880/81. The final episodes take place when she was 17 (see foreword).

[3] This time span is given in a postscript on p. 336 of the manuscript (image on p. iii).

[4] In 1918, poems by Luisa Hewitt and her husband Reginald Mainwaring Hewitt (1887–1948), Professor of English at Nottingham University, appeared in an issue of *Oxford Poetry* alongside works by other Oxford-associated writers, most notably

sent the manuscript to Benjamin Ifor Evans, then Professor of English at the University of Sheffield, and to Basil Blackwell, the prominent Oxford bookseller and publisher.[5] Whereas Blackwell rejected it outright, Evans saw potential in it – were it to be revised: 'I enjoyed it. There is a book in it: but I think you have got to set to work again to get that book out of it. Now curse me if you will!'[6] Hewitt declined the invitation to revise and quietly let the project drop.

More than two decades later, the manuscript had not been forgotten. John Simon Gabriel Simmons, the Taylor Institution's Librarian for Russian and Slavonic, who had a keen interest in the history of the University of Oxford in general and of the Taylorian in particular,[7] was determined not to let Hewitt's autobiography fade into oblivion. Simmons was ultimately responsible for bringing the manuscript to Oxford. In the early 1950s, he corresponded extensively with Hewitt. As she was at first reluctant to part with the original manuscript, Simmons undertook to transcribe selected chapters himself for deposit at the Taylor Institution.

This copy, now held there under the shelfmark MS. 8° E.43, constitutes an editorial version in its own right. In transcribing it, Simmons mostly followed Hewitt's various revisions, yet also made interpretive choices, selecting between alternatives offered by Hewitt and

---

a young Aldous Huxley, see Wilfred R. Childe, Thomas W. Earp and Dorothy L. Sayers (eds), *Oxford Poetry, 1918*. Oxford: B.H. Blackwell, 1918; accessible via gutenberg.org. In addition to that, Luisa and Reginald Hewitt published more of their poetry in a separate volume issued in the same year: Luisa Hewitt and Reginald Mainwaring Hewitt, *Wine and Gall*. Oxford: B.H. Blackwell, 1918. She also used the pen name Elsa Lorraine to publish poetry, see Vivian de Sola Pinto, *Reginald Mainwaring Hewitt (1887–1948). A Selection from His Literary Remains*. Oxford: Printed for the subscribers and distributed by B.H. Blackwell, 1955, p. 10.
[5] For further information on both Benjamin Ifor Evans and Basil Blackwell see their respective entries in the Oxford Dictionary of National Biography (ODNB).
[6] Letter from Benjamin Ifor Evans to Luisa Hewitt, dated 26 January 1932; Taylor Institution Library, MS. 8° E.43; edited in the appendix.
[7] For more detail on his research interests, see Simmons's entry in the ODNB as well as an obituary published in *The Independent* on 23 September 2005.

incorporating marginal insertions. In creating a partial copy of Hewitt's text, Simmons's main concern was not to produce a faithful reproduction of Hewitt's original manuscript. Instead, he aimed to render the text accessible to future readers, expressing his strong belief that 'the historian of the Taylorian writing to celebrate its bicentenary in 2044 would be very pleased to enliven his story from your *Selbstzeugnis!*'[8]

To that end, Simmons compiled a list of pseudonyms, some of which he deduced himself, while others he verified or directly inquired about in correspondence with Hewitt. Unfortunately, not all identities could be established, as considerable time had passed since the manuscript's composition. As a result, some pseudonyms remain undeciphered. Among his other editorial interventions, Simmons also asked Hewitt for a photograph of herself and her father, which he included in the manuscript.[9]

Then as now, readers may wonder whether *The Chronicle* is truly an autobiography or rather a hybrid of fact and fiction. Hewitt herself addressed this question in a letter to Simmons: 'Prof. Evans refused to believe that every word is gospel truth – its only recommendation if it is one. Fact is always stronger if less artistic than Fiction.'[10]

Hewitt eventually donated the typescript[11] to the library in 1952 – three years before she died on 16 October 1955.[12]

---

[8] Letter from Simmons to Hewitt, dated 7 October 1952; Taylor Institution Library MS. 8° E.43 (edited in the appendix).

[9] The photograph of Luisa Hewitt and Heinrich Krebs opens this partial edition.

[10] From Hewitt's letter to Simmons, dated 5 September 5 195[2], Taylor Institution Library MS. 8° E.43 (edited in the appendix).

[11] Now held as Oxford, Bodleian Libraries, MS. Top. Oxon. d. 440. Entry in <u>archives.bodleian.ox.ac.uk</u>.

[12] A short obituary notice appeared in *The Times* on 19 October 1955. A clipping of this notice is held at the Taylor Institution Library under the shelfmark MS. 8° E.43 together with various letters concerning her book and Simmons's partial transcript.

I would like to thank everyone who helped turn Luisa Hewitt's type-script of *The Chronicle of Wisa Dingeldey by Herself* into this published book. Together, we made her wish come true, nearly a century after she sat down at her typewriter to capture memories of her childhood in the Taylor Institution Library in Oxford.

First of all, my sincere gratitude goes to Jill Hughes, former German Subject Librarian at the Taylorian, who first introduced me to Luisa Hewitt's manuscript back in 2017. Ever since, I have wanted to make Hewitt's text available to a broader audience, particularly to the staff and students at the Taylor Institution Library. I am especially grateful to Emma Huber for her tireless support throughout the project: for identifying pseudonyms, matching old plans of the Institution to Luisa Hewitt's descriptions, transcribing some hardly legible hand-writing and coordinating proofreading across the Taylorian's staff. Special thanks are also due to David Hambleton, whose help in lo-cating many of Hewitt's settings was invaluable. I am indebted to him for pointing me to the 1931 building plan and for suggesting the title of this book.

Thank you as well to Catherine Hilliard for being the first reader of this edition and offering helpful insights into the twentieth-century history of the Taylor Institution Library. I would also like to thank Henrike Lähnemann for encouraging me to edit the text and for in-cluding it in *Treasures of the Taylorian* as part of the *Writers in Resi-dence* series – Luisa Hewitt was, after all, very much a resident author!

Finally, my thanks go to Mark Goodhand for offering a home away from home in Oxford and for asking the important question: "Who profits from your work?". I hope that current as well as future stu-dents and library staff will profit from it and that they find as much delight as I did in reading the words of the girl who lived in the library.

This edition is the result of a research stay in Oxford in March and April 2025. Wandering through the building, I tried to match Luisa

Hewitt's descriptions of the Taylor Institution Library at the end of the 19th century to the reality of the building in 2025: her old room, the fireplace on top of which the first librarian supposedly slept on cold nights and the very balcony where the porter once spotted two members of the Alpine Club climbing over the railing for practice, only to watch them slide down the drainpipe when caught. For me, tracing these stories through the library was a joy and I hope you will find just as much pleasure in the pages that follow.

Photograph of the Taylor Institution before the extension of 1932. c1880s, Oxford, Bodleian Libraries, University Archives, TL 5/11

Luisa Hewitt
The Chronicle of Wisa Dingeldey by Herself

The title image shows Heinrich Krebs and his daughter Luisa Hewitt, née Krebs; it is glued on the verso of the manuscript Oxford, Bodleian Libraries, MS. Top. Oxon. d. 440, captioned as 'The autobiographer and her father, ca. 1895'.

This edition is based on the typescript that Hewitt donated to the Bodleian Library in 1952, on the condition that it would not be made publicly accessible for 25 years or before her death, and that a copy of the key chapters concerning the Taylor Institution, namely the copy prepared by John Simon Gabriel Simmons, be held at the Institution itself under the same terms as MS. 8° E.43. Until now, neither the full text nor any excerpts have been published, though some of its anecdotes continue to circulate within the Institution, often without clear knowledge of their source. As Luisa Hewitt's autobiography is an extensive piece of writing, this edition includes only selected parts: two chapters describing life in the Taylor Institution Library and one chapter focusing on her father, his working methods, and his rather peculiar character traits. These are the chapters for which Simmons had prepared a typewritten copy.

In contrast to Simmons's version, this edition preserves the manuscript's impression of a work in progress, as the typescript itself has been revised multiple times – by typewriter, pen and pencil. Where more than one reading is possible, alternatives are provided in the footnotes. Original spelling, capitalisation, underlining and punctuation have been preserved, with additional punctuation added only where necessary for syntactic clarity. The same principle applies to paragraphing. Erroneous repetitions and typographical mistakes have been corrected to enhance the readability of the text.

Hewitt's use of '&' for 'and' has been retained. Wherever she writes in a language other than English, the relevant words have been rendered in italics. Italics are also used for book and magazine titles. All editorial additions and emendations appear in [square brackets].

The following chapters from *The Chronicle of Wisa Dingeldey by Herself* are those Luisa Hewitt allowed Simmons to transcribe for deposit in the Taylor Institution Library.

Front Matter

The former Caretaker's Entrance to the basement of the Taylorian on St Giles
photograph Emma Huber

Front Matter

Terms of Deposit

[p. ii] Mrs L. Hewitt of 63 Orston Drive, Wollaton Park, Nottingham, widow of Professor R[eginald] Hewitt of Nottingham University[1], and daughter of the late Dr H[einrich] Krebs, Librarian of the Taylor Institution, Oxford from 1871 to 1921, places this typescript of her Autobiography in the Bodleian Library on the following conditions:

1. that it be regarded as 'on deposit' in Bodley and subject to withdrawal by the depositor for a period of twenty-five years after the date of deposit, or, until the death of the depositor, whichever be the earlier, and
2. that during the above period no transcripts be made from the typescript nor passages published from it without the consent of the depositor.

A transcript of Chapters 1, 2, and 37 has been placed in the Library of the Taylor Institution on the same conditions.

18 December 1952

---

[1] For a short overview of Reginal Mainwaring Hewitt's life see the entry under his name in https://mss-cat.nottingham.ac.uk/; for a more detailed account see Vivian de Sola Pinto, *Reginald Mainwaring Hewitt (1887–1948). A Selection from His Literary Remains*. Oxford: Printed for the subscribers and distributed by B.H. Blackwell, 1955, pp. 1–44, especially p. 10f.

List of Pseudonyms

PSEUDONYMS

(Elucidations by Mrs Hewitt)

MS. Top. Oxon. d. 440, p. iii
List of pseudonyms compiled by John Simon Gabriel Simmons

[p. iii][2] Basil Street: Broad Street
Mr Bloggs: Mr Higgs, perhaps of Balliol[3]
Major Campbell: Mr Gordon[4]
The Chase: The Parks
Coverley's College: Magdalen
Dingeldey: Krebs
Fairminster: Oxford
Fletcher Street: Beaumont Street
Gabriel Fields: Christ Church Meadows
Great Orange Street: High Street
Guardians: Curators (of the Taylor Institution)
Halle, Professor Hans: Professor Max Müller[5]

---

[2] Simmons added pages iii and iv to the manuscript before placing it in the Bodleian, in accordance with Hewitt's request, and labelled it 'Elucidations by Mrs Hewitt'. Only those pseudonyms relevant to the edited chapters below are transcribed here.

[3] Arthur Hibble Higgs was an undergraduate student at Balliol College from 1871 to 1874, see the Oxford History website.

[4] Mr Gordon cannot be further identified – he was a regular visitor at the library, see p. 354 of the manuscript.

[5] Friedrich Max Müller (1823–1900) was the Taylor Institution's second Professor of Modern European Languages and, from 1868, Oxford University's first Professor of Comparative Philology. John R. Davis and Angus Nicholls, 'Friedrich Max Müller: The Career and Intellectual Trajectory of a German Philologist in Victorian Britain', *Publications of the English Goethe Society*, 85.2–3 (2016), pp. 67–97. Lourens P. van den Bosch, *Friedrich Max Müller. A Life Devoted to Humanities*. Leiden: Brill, 2002. Christina Ostermann and Henrike Lähnemann, 'Friedrich Max Müller and the Acquisition of Reformation Pamphlets at the Taylor Institution Library'. In: *Forum for*

Ilex Alley: perhaps Magpie Lane
Lemon Street: Longwall
Dr Lloyd-Lloyd: Mr Llewellyn (father-in-law of Mr Hurst, Dr Krebs's Assistant)
Mezzofanti: Taylor Institution
Mintham: Binsey
Mouseaton: Hinksey
Nimrod College: Balliol
Mr Page the bookbinder: Mr Morley
Periclean Museum: Ashmolean
Pretenders' Pillar: Martyrs' Memorial
Pryce & Pritchard: Thomas (chemist in Magdalen St., opposite St Mary Magdalen Church)
Rueville: Summertown
Rye Mart: Cornmarket
Sageby: Cumnor
St Joseph's Street: St John's Street
[p. iv] St Lambert's Street: St Giles
St Perkin's Church: St Mary Magdalen[e]
Simnel Road: Woodstock Road
Duckworth Swann: Robert Finch[6]
Timonden: Marston
Warbeck Road: Banbury Road
Wells: Clifford (porter of the Taylorian ?1895–?1915).
His predecessor, 'Old Evans', was porter from ?1875–?1895.
Professor Baker White: Professor Cook Wilson[7]
Wykeham Mound College: New College

Modern Language Studies. Special Issue: Migration Collections: Translocation Research in Libraries and Archives, 1850–2025. Ed. by Sophia Buck and Stefanie Hundehege (forthcoming 2026).
[6] Robert Finch (1783–1830), an alumnus of the University of Oxford, directed in his will that his extensive collection of books and art be left to the Taylor Institution. His estate also established the Finch Fund for additional acquisitions.
[7] John Cook Wilson (1849–1915), philosopher and Oxford alumnus, became Wykeham Professor of Logic at the University of Oxford in 1889.

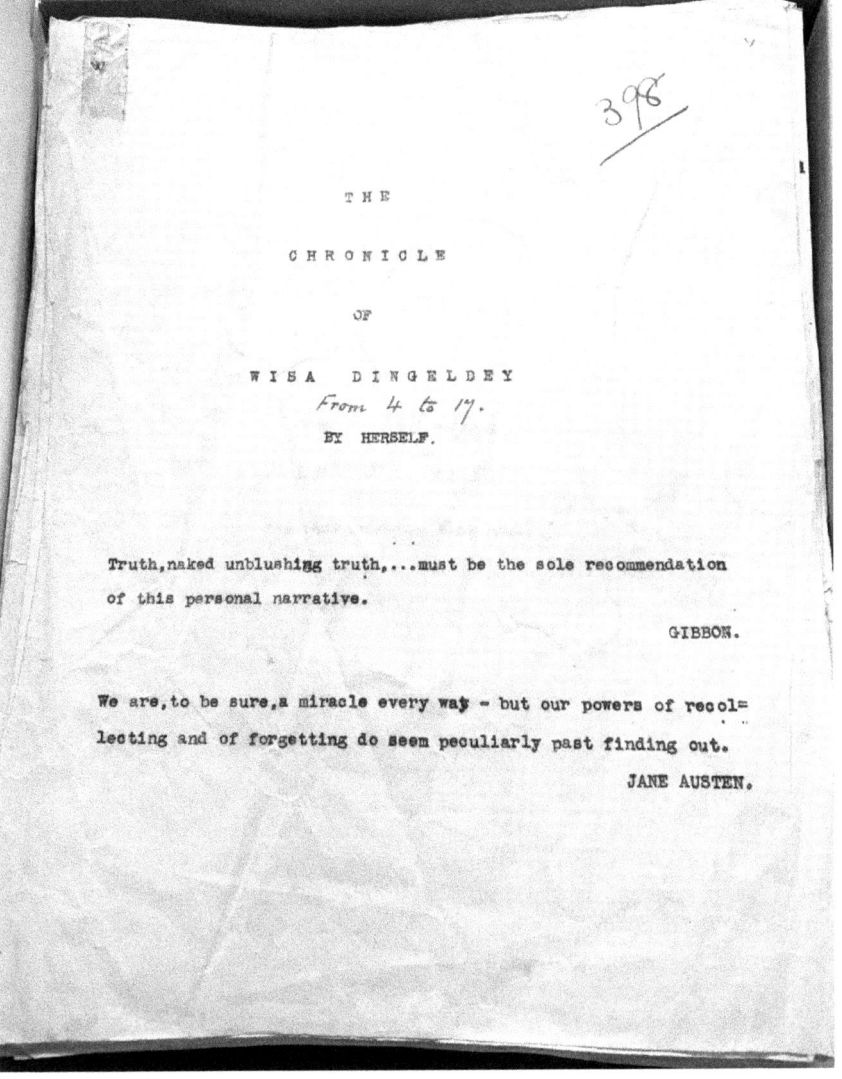

THE

CHRONICLE

OF

WISA   DINGELDEY

From 4 to 17.

BY   HERSELF.

Truth,naked unblushing truth,...must be the sole recommendation
of this personal narrative.

GIBBON.

We are,to be sure,a miracle every way - but our powers of recol=
lecting and of forgetting do seem peculiarly past finding out.

JANE AUSTEN.

MS. Top. Oxon. d. 440, Title page

Title Page

The Chronicle of Wisa[8] Dingeldey by Herself
From 4 to 17[9]

> Truth, naked unblushing truth, ... must be the sole recommendation of this personal narrative.
> Gibbon.[10]

> We are, to be sure, a miracle every way – but our powers of recollecting and of forgetting do seem peculiarly past finding out.
> Jane Austen.[11]

Dedication

To Joye in Fiji who bade me write this book.

HHHHHHHHHHHHHHHHHHHHHHHHHHHHHHHHHH
XXXXXXXXXXXXXXXXXXXXXXXXXXXXXXXXXX
HHHHHHHHHHHHHHHHHHHHHHHHHHHHHHHHHH

---

[8] Letters of condolence sent to Hewitt after her husband's death show that 'Wisa' was her real-life nickname, see the following record in the University of Nottingham's Manuscripts and Special Collections Online Catalogue.

[9] Added below in handwritten ink. This addition narrows the timespan given in the foreword: 'from the age of three approximately to the age of seventeen'.

[10] From the opening paragraph of the autobiography of Oxford-educated historian Edward Gibbon, *Memoirs of Edward Gibbon, Written by Himself, and a Selection from His Letters*. Ed. by John Holroyd Sheffield and Henry Morley. London: G. Routledge, 1891; p. 35; even more so than Luisa Hewitt, Gibbon was critical of his time at Oxford, see p. 66: 'To the University of Oxford I acknowledge no obligation and she will as cheerfully renounce me for a son as I am willing to disclaim her for a mother. I spent fourteen months at Magdalen College; they proved the fourteen months the most idle and unprofitable of my whole life.'

[11] Jane Austen, *Mansfield Park*. Ed. by James Kinsley. Oxford: OUP, 2020, p. 163.

Contents

CONTENTS.

PAGE
CHAPTER
1 THE BIG ROOM   1
2 THE LIBRARY   10

MS. Top. Oxon. d. 440, p. vii (Contents)

Foreword

[p. ix] The following is a true and accurate account of all that I remember to have seen and done and felt from the age of three approximately to the age of seventeen. Detailed and minute in parts like a pen & ink drawing, it will prove tedious to the reader who is out for accident rather than for incident, and I crave the pardon of such. On the other hand I flatter myself in offering as sincere an impression as I am able; and the contrast between German & English life, chiefly in schools it is true, but to a certain extent outside of them, is bound to be an utterly unbiased one since I can truly count myself as belonging to both or to neither of these nations, and have no patriotic axe to grind in blessing or cursing them.

If in these pages I have given undue prominence to the appearance of people, especially of those who did not please me, if I have made too many hasty & unkind reflections, I wish to disclaim responsibility for them at this date. Children are slaves to externals; my judgments have necessarily softened in the space of forty years, and I am confident that they would be very different now about the people I knew then, since not I alone but they too will have changed. If any should happen to recognise themselves under fictitious names, I hope they will be lenient where I have been malicious. Let them feel sure that they could repay spite with spite if they had it in them, but that they are too well-bred, or have at any rate forgotten me. [p. x] As far as possible I give the actual impressions made on me at the time of which I am writing. My expressions are of to-day; my feelings[1] those of forty years ago.

The portrait of my father I had not the heart to curtail within the limits of thirteen years. The anecdotes are mostly of his latter period of his life at Fairminster, from 1900 to 1921, when he returned to Germany.   Nottingham, 28 May, 1931

---

[1] A specification added in typescript below reads: 'my feelings described'.

Chapter 1: The Big Room

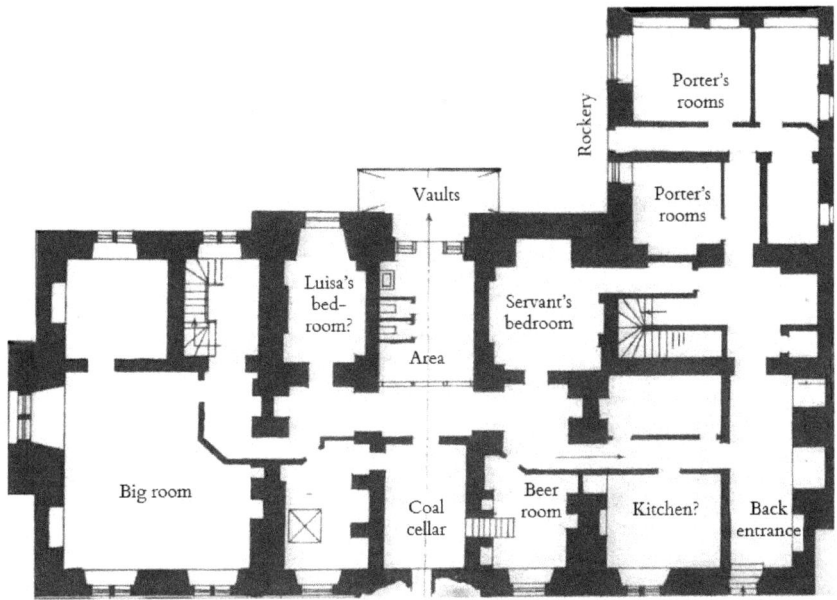

Plan of the basement according to Luisa Hewitt
Labels by Christina Ostermann and Emma Huber

[p. 1] The "Big Room" as it was called, a bare & unattractive, sunless kind of barn, where I was born, hardly deserved its share of the romantic halo surrounding the Mezzofanti Library.[2] Later it always appeared to me ironic that friends should envy me the privilege of living & breathing there. The Mezzofanti was a building of Greek proportions in the University town of Fairminster. How stately & glorious from without! How dismal & undwellable within, only the tenants, ourselves & the porter knew. He was a widower in my mother's days, & congratulated himself on that fact in his talks with her. "Ah, Mrs. Dingeldey," he would say, "this ain't a fit place to bring up a family in; it's these damp, sweaty passages as 'as give me

---

[2] For a comparison of how the locations of Luisa's childhood relate to the modern layout, refer to the plans in the appendix.

my rheumatism." Not a very encouraging remark to make to a bride. The same old porter once observed to my father, "The sparrow's a knowing bird in this country!" a joke elementary enough for Papa fully to savour.[3] A third remark handed down to me was: "Well, I've never seen a child as was fonder of salt than of sugar!" This [occurred] when[,] invited to tea in his room[,] I serenely went on helping myself to salt, either from a mistake in impression that it was sugar, or from a real preference. Though, possibly even at two or three years old a stubborn pride of persistence mingled with the dread of ridicule may have actuated me.

My father took the comfortless suite of apartments allotted him with at least outward philosophy; one never knew what he felt. Like a dog he seemed at times susceptible to ease & luxury when supplied by others; he appreciated the elegance of a tastefully furnished house, & would cosily bask in a deep armchair at someone else's fire-side. It never occurred [to him] to go & furnish likewise. His parsimony, bred in the bone, made him unwilling [p. 2] to spend a halfpenny on a daily paper; much less wo[u]ld he dream of spending pounds on furniture. Moreover his dwelling was not his own; which combined with his intention of returning to Germany in the near future – a plan of which he never lost sight for a single moment[4] – in making him loth to contribute to the greater comfort & convenience of his family.

---

[3] The porter possibly refers to the poem *Vulture, Sparrow, and Birds* by John Gay (1685–1732). In the final stanza, the sparrow voices a preference for a simple life over ambition or wealth: 'A sparrow, on the housetop, heard | The sparrow is a knowing bird: | If rogues unto preferments rise, | I ask nor place nor seignories. | To the thatched cottage, I, to find, | From courts afar, my peace of mind.'.

[4] Yet a plan which was put in place at a very late point in time: Heinrich Krebs worked as librarian at the Taylor Institution in Oxford from 1871 to 1921, the year he returned to Germany and passed away. On p. 366f., Hewitt writes: 'He died shortly after the Great Peace, at Darmstadt, in a Franciscan Hospital; his desire, that of retiring to his native town having been granted him, but for how brief an interval; he only drew one quarter's pension.'

So the barn remained a barn, inadequately & as it were provisionally furnished by the Guardians of the Library, who without doubt expected my father to contribute the rest. There was a small Turkey square[5] from one of the lecture rooms, which in the process of time became shabbier & shabbier, around which the bare & splintered boards were always ready to be scrubbed. Still, in those days, there must have been a surround of Brussels[6], for I subsequently met remnants of the same; & things would look less cheerless than twenty years after. In spite of his constant remark about retiring "next year," my father lived here for the space of forty years or more, marrying in the ninth year after his appointment[7].

Of the pictures on the walls of the Big Room I only remember two: one was a highly coloured specimen of the Surrender at Sedan, a wedding-present from Papa's dentist. A sheepish looking Napoleon III handing over his sword to an extremely bourgeois Kaiser Wilhelm. The second picture displayed the English Royal Family before Victoria's grandmaternal days. She sits in matronly complacence,[8] encircled by girls & boys in their teens; the boys in white sailor suits, the girls with sashes & ribbons. Every Christmas during my childhood an old gentleman gave Papa *Pear's Annual*[9] for me; the loose picture appended was pinned on the wall over the horsehair sopha; the [p. 3] old one, dusty & devoid of further interest being taken down to make room for it. I well recollect my excitement in unrolling the new picture [–] what would it be this time? [A]nimal, child, or lovely lady with gentleman? [O]nce there were several ladies ... three, to be exact, leaning over a river wall or bridge, in bland

---

[5] Turkish square rug.

[6] 'Brussels' is short for 'Brussels carpet': 'A kind of carpet having a back of stout linen thread and an upper surface of wool', see OED, *Brussels carpet (n.)*.

[7] That is in 1880, not long before Luisa was born.

[8] 'wreathed by' is crossed out as Hewitt opted for 'encircled by'.

[9] *Pears' Annual* was an illustrated magazine published by the company *Pears Soap* from 1891 until 1925. It combined art, literature and advertising and was popular as a gift and collectible, especially around Christmas, see https://eghammuseum.org/ and the Encyclopedia of Science Fiction.

intercourse with a sailor below; they were all so beautiful in my eyes that I could never decide to which to give the preference, brunette, blonde or black.

But the really unpleasant feature of the Big Room, afterwards looming in my mind as a squalid secret, of which I felt as deeply ashamed as if it had been an abnormal vice of my own self, was that it so blatantly suggested sleeping & dressing rather than sitting & eating. A tall fire-guard, introduced for safety while I was small, & regarded afterwards by Papa as a fixture, never to be even temporarily removed, shut off the tiny grate from the enormous room; an iron double bedstead filling the space between two windows facing East was surrounded by a clumsy screen, covered with an ugly varnished paper. [N]ear it, in one corner stood a marble washstand, blatantly in view; in the other corner a high chest of drawers with all the appointments of a dressing-table took as little trouble as the washstand to hide its face: naked & unabashed they joined issue with the square leather & mahogany writing table used for dining, in the middle of the room. Two bookcases & a wardrobe, four library chairs with leather seats, that matched the table, & a horsehair couch & armchair supplied perforce by my father completed the effects. Opposite the door was a third window that faced south, & at right angles with it a door led into an inner room that remained unfurnished for years but was always left wide open.[10] The three grated windows of the Big Room could only be reached by climbing up a moveable stepladder that stood there for the purpose.

[p. 4] The window recesses, twice the height of the frames & only half filled by these, were like small balconies, & might have been furnished as miniature boudoirs. Some £50 spent on the Barn (as Mrs. Benson, Papa's last housekeeper consistently called it) would have made it inhabitable, & in later years I used to amuse or console

---

[10] Here, it becomes clear that the 'Big Room' refers to the space nowadays known as the 'Celtic Collection and Slavonic Research Collection' in the Taylorian's basement, see the modern basement plan in the appendix.

myself with planning imaginary schemes of furnishing it. I did, as a fact, spend a good deal of my slender dress allowance on items of drapery, stools, cushions etc. to relieve the general dinginess, which a few rays of the morning sun that fell through unwillingly as it were, but served to intensify.

What made this habitation so impracticable was that the other rooms – for there were such – had not been designed by the builder with any idea to convenience, or apparently with any idea at all. They might & did ultimately serve the purpose of storing an overflow of books & periodicals;[11] meanwhile they lay so remote from one another that three or four mutual enemies could have lived in them respectively without being incommoded. The basement kitchen was on a level, it is true, with the dining-room (Big Room); but separated by the length of a straggling stone passage; midway down which a door on one hand led to a coal-cellar, & on the other hand to an area.[12] A little further, at a turn of the passage, two doors, again on either hand, opened into the servant's bedroom & a small room known as the beer-room, the origin of which name I will presently explain. So that hot viands carried along here would have plenty of opportunity to cool. The area I referred to gave on to a sort of underground – in this case undergarden – cellar or cave, consisting of three vaults in which the ashes of a whole twelvemonth were allowed to accumulate; the sanitary inspector remaining in blissful ignorance of this state of affairs[13]. [p. 5] In the nearest of the three vaults, the one & only lavatory was situated; here the walls oozed & dripped in damp weather, & the flags shone & perspired. If you turned to the right of the entrance to the vaults, you came to a pleasant rockery faced by the porter's windows; friendly lace curtains & geraniums or

---

[11] This is exactly what the basement is primarily used for today: storing books and periodicals.

[12] The locations of the rooms mentioned here and in the following are marked on the annotated basement plan in the appendix.

[13] The last typed word on this page, presumably 'that', has been struck through in ink with 'this state of affairs' added in handwriting in the bottom margin.

winter cherries converted this corner of the building to homeliness. I could not wander here, it was private; yet often as a child & even later I perversely longed to penetrate to the farthest corner of that raised rockery. To the left of the vaults, the area ran on for another few yards or so, coming to a stop at a blank wall below the street. At right angles to this wall was the window of the little room leading out of the Big Room, opposite which was a grated door kept permanently closed. I used to picture all sorts of weird things behind this door, although I knew, for I had persuaded Sarah[14] or someone to open it just once, that it was a vault similar to the familiar ones beyond, & contained nothing, not even ashes. Nothing except the Dark. And so after my first momentary disappointment, I might still people or fill it with hidden treasure, to my heart's terror & content. To reach the porter's rooms, of which you have seen the windows, you passed our kitchen, turned a sharp corner through another straggling passage, & at the next bend you stood between the back door, his entrance, on your right, & his dwelling on your left. I believe we had a right to use this entrance, at any rate my father often did; but I had a feeling that the porter did not like us to use it. Though that was not in the time of old Wells. He would have welcomed anything on our part that savoured of taking a liberty; whereas his more youthful successor, a retired soldier of the Indian army, bore a glum & sullen demeanour, as well as being stupid to excess: Papa sometimes said of him [p. 6] when they had annoyed one another, "One might batter in walls with him." A German proverb, signifying the hardness of his skull.[15]

---

[14] Sarah is not mentioned in Simmons's list of pseudonyms. On p. 357, she is identified as the first of Heinrich Krebs's three housekeepers over his fifty years as librarian.

[15] The proverb referred to here is '*Man könnte Wände mit ihm einrennen*', see Karl F. W. Wander (ed.), *Deutsches Sprichwörter-Lexikon.* Leipzig: N.p., 1867, vol. 4, p. 1778, Nr. 55 – the explanation matches Hewitt's own: '*so dumm (hartköpfig) ist er*' (that is how stupid (stubborn) he is).

19th century boot scraper next to the St Giles entrance
photograph Emma Huber

The passages were paved with lead-coloured flags, which, like the ones outside, perspired so freely on rainy days that they appeared to have been scoured by pouring buckets of water over them & leaving them to dry at leisure.

More than 120 wide stone steps, permanently uncarpeted, led to the top of the building; on each of the three successive floors, there was one room. The first, on a level with the entrance door (Librarian's) & situated in a semi-porch or hall which led also to a lecture-room[16], had all the appearance of being a segment of the aforesaid lecture-

---

[16] This lecture room is nowadays known as the 'Voltaire Room' (or 'Room 1'), see also the description of this room by Giles Barber in 'A Continuing Tradition: Non-Book Materials in the Taylor Institution Library'. In: *Bodleian Library Record* 17.3–4 (2001), pp. 261–267, here p. 263f.: "Lecture Room 1 was formerly decorated in High Victorian style, possibly following the advice of the architect, C. S. Cockerell, an expert on the interior decoration of Greek temples. Formerly it contained a pulpit-like rostrum, and even now, reassigned as a reading room, it retains its architectural features, the upper wall panels still having the original frescoes in the Parthenon manner and the University arms on the ceiling".

room. It was of the same height, about twenty feet, & disproportion-
ately minute in ground space; besides, a green baize door in the room
turned out to be a way into the lecture room. This segment of it,
which was our drawing-room[17], I always longed to lay on its side;
for it was a heartbreaking task to make it look anything but odd.

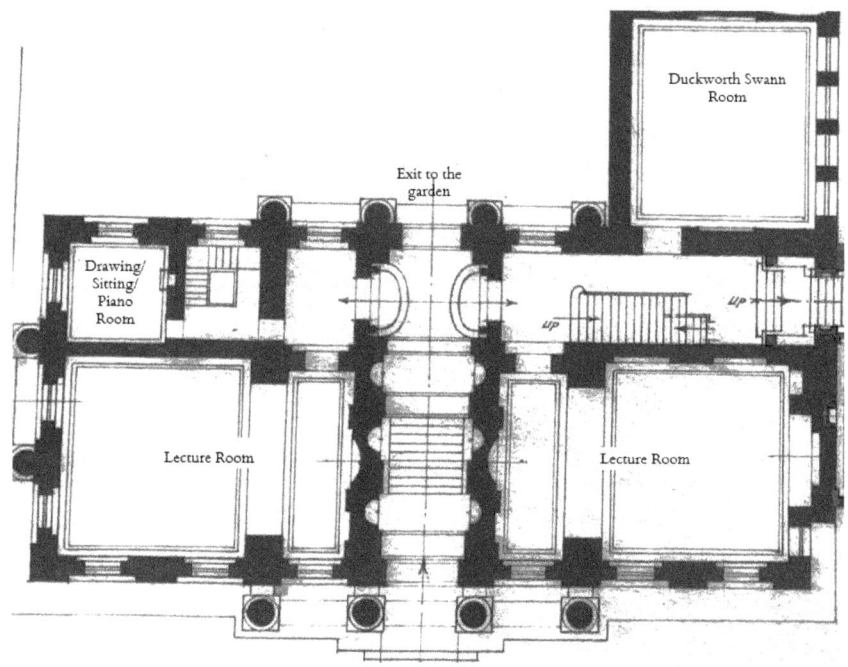

Ground floor of the Taylorian according to Luisa Hewitt
Labels by Emma Huber and Christina Ostermann

In my mother's day, it had no doubt a certain Victorian dignity with
its plum-coloured paper stamped with white diamonds, its heavy
green brocade & plum rep[18] hangings. The curtains hung one set

---

[17] The drawing room is nowadays used as a staff office, see the modern plan of the
ground floor in the appendix.
[18] The Oxford English Dictionary defines 'rep' as: 'A plain-weave fabric (usually of
wool, silk, or cotton) with a ribbed surface, used esp. for draperies and upholstery',
see OED *rep* (n. & adj.).

above the other; & I remember wondering, when they first attracted my notice, why there were two short instead of one long pair. Even now I can only account for this from the inconvenience it would have caused any two persons to shake & fold such a double length. The two immense windows nearly five feet from the ground but stretching up immeasurably, faced one towards Fletcher Street & the other towards the garden exposed to that street[.] These windows let in all the dust & draught of an extremely noisy thoroughfare. They were nearly always, particularly the one on the [p. 7] street, coated & dimmed with grime, being cleaned from the outside only once a year. In this room, known as the Sitting-room, though nobody ever sat there for long at a time, my parents at rare intervals entertained friends[19] to tea; it being obviously, for reasons already stated, impossible to invite them to a meal in the basement. Here in the Segment, then, my mother would sometimes, accompanying herself on her piano, sing such songs as "Ruth", "The Better Land", "Sun of my Soul" (a setting secularised by variations),[20] & of course many German classical & traditional songs. One of these was called "The Cuckoo"[21], & its refrain was a question to that prophetic bird, as to how many more years the singer had to live.

"Ach, nur ein Jahr oder zwei?"
"Kukuk, das ist zu bald!"

---

[19] 'friends' typed over another word, most probably 'guests'.

[20] Thanks to Henrike Lähnemann for identifying these songs: The first is most likely *Ruth – A Sacred Song,* edited by Fred. Lyster, with music by Miss Davis, see the scan in the Berkeley Library. The second perhaps *The Better Land* by Mrs Hemans and Frederic H. Cowen, published in 1878, see the scan in the Library of Congress. The third might be the hymn *Sun of my soul. Thou Saviour dear* written by John Keble (1819–1885) in 1820, see hymnary.org.

[21] The song in question is *Sage mir, Vogel im grünen Wald* (Tell me bird, in the green forest) by Franz Abt (1819–1885), Op. 237 No. 4. Thanks to Johanna Ziemann (Zentrum für Populäre Kultur und Musik, University of Freiburg) for identifying this piece and for her helpful comments on the widespread superstition that a cuckoo foretells a person's remaining years of life.

(What, only one year or two? Cuckoo, that is too soon!) [M]y mother sang probably on a Sunday evening, that being the only day on which a fire was afforded here. Probably too the cuckoo clock, more dateless & alive[22] than its Victorian room-mates, would join in, & that did not matter.

Her[23] voice would have to battle, as mine in later years, with the clamour outside, of the Salvation Army, of too many church bells, & of several prophets, all of whom chose the same spot from which to shout their revelations, namely the Pretender's Pillar. For the Mezzofanti stands, as you are aware, at the busiest corner of St. Lambert's Street, one side towards Fletcher Street, but looking on the other across to the Pillar, & St. Perkin's Church, & comprising even Nimrod College Corner in its view. But the third side of the wing – the Library was after all only a wing of the Periclean Museum – gave less uncompromisingly on the street. It showed a formal lawn [p. 8] which sloped up to a terrace on either side of the main gates, towards Fletcher Street. On this terrace – on ours, that is to say, for the entrance divided it in two & the other belonged to the Periclean Museum – there stood a solitary laburnum, & a little further off, a lilac bush my father had planted in one of his first years; the lilac flowered & flourished exceedingly, aided no doubt by the daily buckets of soapy bath water he applied year by year it became more of a protest against the conventional lawn, a suggestion of happy-go-lucky nature in the austere design. One summer an artist begged to be allowed to do a painting of this aggressively exuberant shrub; & Papa, encouraged by the compliment, had the audacity in the following autumn to plant an apple tree & then a cherry-tree in conspicuous positions (but all positions were equally so) upon the lawn. The Guardians very pardonably drew the line at this, & he had to relinquish his fruit-trees! The laburnum was of untold use & comfort as a shelter from the street on the otherwise public terrace; even so, the

---

[22] One word before 'alive' crossed out and rendered illegible.
[23] 'But' before 'Her' crossed out.

windows of the great Churchill Hotel[24] opposite, like so many hundreds of eyes, I fancied, were staring down on me as I stood leaning against the stone balustrade & watched the passersby; though still more interesting it was to see the visitors at the Hotel, going in & out, arriving & departing, by hansom cab and fourwheel in those days; or when the carpet was laid outside & on the steps for some reception or dance or grand wedding & a little crowd would gather[25] to see the carriages roll up, & the daintily shod feet in gold or silver below clouds of gauze & tulle & shimmering satin glide up & through to unknown pleasures often pictured by me in my half-hiding-place below the laburnum.

[p. 9] Yet I may have envied even more than these the head porter in his goldlaced coat with the burnished buttons. He had nothing to do but stand or sit in the porch, & open carriage doors. As for the tips I have seen him receive with such mechanical unconcern they must have filled his coffers long ago, to say nothing of those I have *not* seen him receive. He is still in office, but very old & bent.

But to return to the Mezzofanti Library. On the floor above the sitting-room or as Papa preferred to call it, the piano-room there was a replica of it, another segment, this time of the Guardians' Assembly Room[26], the handsomest room in the building, which I shall have occasion to describe later. This top room of ours stood empty until I was eleven, when Papa migrated there to sleep. He disliked changes of any kind, but after an attack of asthma, the doctor recommended him to vacate the basement for something airier; to go up, in fact, as high as possible. He might have climbed yet further, to an attic with

---

[24] Simmons did not include the Churchill Hotel in the list of pseudonyms. It is clear, however, that what is meant here is the Randolph Hotel on Beaumont Street that was opened in 1866 and operates to the present day.

[25] Final 'er' and a semicolon added in handwritten ink, the latter of which has not been included in the rendition of the text above to keep the syntax intact.

[26] The location of this room is marked in the annotated plan of the first floor in the appendix. It is nowadays used as the French and German Reading Room. The segment mentioned is now the Librarian's office.

two portholes under the eaves; but here the ceiling was low enough to touch, & that would hardly have answered the purpose. From the aforesaid room however he was able with ease to pass into the library itself.

Main Reading Room of the Taylorian with the portrait of Sir Robert Taylor above the fireplace, the clock, and the busts of Robert Finch and his father Thomas
Photograph Henrike Lähnemann

Chapter 2: The Library

[p. 10] The library was a room of noble dimensions, alternately intersected with high windows of a proportionate width & grated bays of bookshelves filled with elegantly bound books.[27] A gallery ran round the roof, to which an iron spiral stair gave access from below; this gallery was also lined with books & lit by four semicircular windows, one at each corner[28] & containing seats: they were the arches of the windows below, thus broken by the gallery. Two doors up a few more steps led to the attics of which I spoke & which for the most part contained tomes of bound newspapers & journals, all in foreign languages.[29] Two doors in the library itself led respectively to the Guardians' Committee Room & to a lecture room[30] lined also throughout with books: it was really an annex of the library, in which lectures & coachings could sometimes be held by courtesy & in case of an overflow. The lecture halls[31] proper were on the ground floor[32], down a wide staircase of stone, removed from our private one by the full breadth & length of the library.[33] The upstairs lecture room was furnished with hard chairs & long tables on which lay inviting sheets of pink blotting paper & attractive quills, one of which Papa would

---

[27] What follows here is an accurate description of the Main Reading Room of the Taylor Institution Library, which remains virtually unchanged to this day.

[28] The total number of semicircular windows is in fact six. In addition to the ones in each corner, there is one in the middle of the east and west side of the room, see the plan of the second floor in the appendix.

[29] Today, one of these two rooms serves as the Graduate Study Room and the other as a staff room; see the gallery level plan in the appendix.

[30] The Guardians' Committee Room – or Guardians' Assembly Room, as Hewitt later refers to it – is now known as the French and German Reading Room, while the lecture room referred to here corresponds to today's Enquiry Room.

[31] 'halls' typed over another word, possibly 'rooms'.

[32] 'down below' crossed out before 'on the ground floor'.

[33] The three lecture halls on the ground floor are nowadays known as the Voltaire Room, Room 2 and Room 3 (the latter also known as the Slavonic Reading Room).

sometimes, very rarely though, abstract for me with as great a reluc-
tance as if he had actually to pull it from the fretful porcupine[34]. The
prevailing colour of the furniture was yellow ..[.] it was either New
Zealand pine or, quite probably, good oak, excruciatingly stained &
varnished; even in my early days the colour struck me as ugly in
wood & out of harmony with the rest.

Over the immense bronze & marble fireplace loomed a recess wide
enough to hold a mattress; in fact, a former librarian had slept there,
so he [p. 11] informed my father & found it exceedingly pleasant
with the giant fire ebbing for hours beneath him.[35] In the recess[36]
there hung a portrait of the founder[37], a benevolent image enough to
my childish eyes, & in the fire beneath it I built cities & beheld vi-
sions, even among the desert of embers, to which I would creep at
night, for they gave out the warmth of an ordinary living fire of a
normal size. Often have I stayed to watch the last glow die, while
around me the shadows deepened – such distant shadows, some of
them – and I pretended to myself that ghosts or fairies or other untold
forces undreamt of in my philosophy for I was really somewhat scep-
tical, hovered in the darkness they were, as far as I conceived them
not malevolent. Only sometimes there overcame me a feeling of
space & vast aloneness when I became conscious of the stone corridors & staircases beyond the great doors, & of the silence there, so
productive of echoes, but stretching away unbroken then.

---

[34] 'fretful porcupine' refers to Shakespeare's use of 'fretful porpentine' in *Hamlet*,
i.5.20, see William Shakespeare, *The New Oxford Shakespeare: Modern Critical Edition*. Ed. by Gary Taylor et al. Oxford: Oxford University Press, 2016, p. 2017.

[35] Heinrich Krebs's predecessor was John Macray, who took up the post in 1847,
two years before the library officially opened. The fireplace – though no longer in
use for health and safety reasons – remains a feature in the Main Reading Room
today.

[36] 'On the wall' crossed out before 'In the recess'.

[37] The portrait still hangs over the fireplace in the Main Reading Room and indeed
shows the founder of the institution, Sir Robert Taylor (1714–1788). The painting
is attributed to William Miller and dates from around 1782/83, see artuk.org.

In the Assembly Room, where the Guardians met in order to discuss the purchase of new books & other library affairs there hung a portrait less congenial to me than the old gentleman in the library; it was that of a stern-faced Master of Arts in full academicals, who was connected in some way with the Mezzofanti: it may have been Duckworth Swann, the donor of the Swann Collection of 18th Century books, but I am not sure.[38] My father, carrying me round the library, as was his custom on Sunday afternoons or on a weekday after closing hours, would point him out to me as we passed; by way of reproof, as a kind of bogey, when I had been naughty, or warningly when I had not. I grew to be intensely in awe of this portrait, & scarcely dared to look in its direction when entering the room. Halfway up the wrought iron staircase I used to halt & fancy [p. 12] myself suspended between heaven & earth as on a Jacob's ladder. There was fascination in that spiral staircase, fascination too in the perpetual glimmer of the incandescent lights below the ceiling. I dimly recollect the introduction of this circle of gas, to supersede what must have been hanging oil lamps, though they left no impression on me[.] Like the shrine-lamp in the vault of a cathedral the new lights burned, everlastingly dim but steady, except when after sunset a full illumination was desired. Then the words "DOMINUS ILLUMINATIO MEA"[39] written upon the roof stood out more clearly; but whether He was able to do so entirely remains doubtful, since although the whole library lay bathed in a soft light that picked out the bright covers of the volumes favoured by Professor Paul Canterbury (who always advocated the most showy & costly bindings)[40], & the

---

[38] The painting mentioned here could not be identified. It is not part of the present-day equivalent to the Guardians' Assembly Room, the French and German Reading Room.

[39] The motto of the University of Oxford and the beginning of Psalm 27. Both the Voltaire Room and Room 2 still feature the university's coat of arms and the motto as part of the ceiling decoration, though not the Main Reading Room.

[40] Simmons did not include 'Professor Paul Canterbury' in his list of pseudonyms. From the context provided here, it can be assumed that he was a member of the Curators (or 'Guardians', as Hewitt refers to them). At the end of the 19th century,

few readers' faces were lit up too, yet it must have been difficult to decipher the printed page by that kindly far-off gleam. Gas-brackets were introduced at a later period & placed at lower angles.[41]

The university coat of arms on the ceiling of the Voltaire Room
Photograph Henrike Lähnemann

To indicate closing time the porter would come in at 5 minutes to 5; he busied himself raking here, extinguishing there & bringing in the afternoon post of books & papers. No bell was rung but his presence did succeed in suggesting to more sensitive readers that they had better go; to the more absorbed he murmured: "Closing now, Sir",

the Curators consisted of nine members. The Vice-Chancellor, the Regius Professor of Modern History, and the Professor of Comparative Literature were standing members. These three nominated an additional six, whose appointments had to be confirmed by Convocation, see the Bodleian website. Among the elected members during the period covered in this autobiography (1885–1897/98) were Friedrich Max Müller – whom Hewitt gave the pseudonym 'Hans Halle' – and Edward Moore, Principal of St Edmund Hall and a renowned Dante scholar. The latter was also a noted bibliophile, whose extensive book collection now forms part of the Taylor Institution's special collections. Given his well-documented passion for rare books, it is possible that Moore is the figure behind the pseudonym 'Paul Canterbury'.

[41] The sentence originally opened with 'A little later', but this phrase has been crossed out as Hewitt went for a different syntactic structure.

"Closing, five o'clock, Madam," & having seen them off the premises he exchanged a remark or two with Papa, addressed me as "Missie" & locked one or two doors to which my father had keys of his own. This porter was the battering-ram of whom I spoke in the last chapter: not old Wells of my mother's time, of whom I have but the haziest image in my mind. As soon as the porter had gone, my father wound up the black marble clock[42] on the white marble mantelpiece (the bed of his [p. 13] predecessor), cleared away books & put back chairs forgotten by the porter in their exact places, & attended to other similar matters. One of these was to see that all the windows which led[43] on to narrow balconies were secured; in this he was particularly scrupulous, for once to his amazement & dismay he had encountered two men in the act of swinging themselves over the parapet. When he enquired their business, they amazed him still further by vanishing down the drainpipe, which probably dismayed him not at all. On reporting to the Guardians it transpired that it was not burglars but members of the Alpine Club who had paid him a visit.

I must have been seven or eight years old when I began to accompany Papa on his evening round; he would bend down & let me climb on his back, whence I surveyed the kingdom of vast rooms & halls & corridors with a sense of possessive power. When he had been through all of them I insisted on riding round & round the library proper; four times round was the usual limit. "Three for a boy, & four for a girl" he would say. Or else it was seven times, seven being a sacred number; but of course never as many times as I could have wished. On one of these occasions he pointed to a tiny[44] crescent of light in one corner of the gallery, the North West corner it was –

---

[42] This black marble clock still stands in exactly the same location as described here; for a photograph see the Bodleian blog. Giles Barber, librarian at the Taylor Institution from 1970 to 1996, notes: "The fine black marble clock over the fireplace is by Charles Frodsham of Paris", Giles Barber, 'A Continuing Tradition: Non-Book Materials in the Taylor Institution Library'. In: *Bodleian Library Record* 17.3–4 (2001), pp. 261–267, here p. 264.

[43] 'looked' crossed out before 'led'.

[44] 'small' struck through and 'tiny' added above in handwritten ink.

"See there." he whispered, "that is the angel shadow!".. And he told me that it was my mother watching over us.[45] I was moderately thrilled & after this regularly looked out for the "Engelschatten", whether alone or with him. Some nights it did not appear & I fancy now that it must have been some sky effect, an "error of the moon", most likely. I do not think I ever believed it to be my mother's spirit; for it never moved & I thought she would have given some sign & not met our interest with complete indifference. [p. 14] Once, in a fit of exuberance, I grew insolent. Using my knees as spurs I bid my bearer "*Hopp, hopp, alter Esel!*" (Gee-up, old ass!) Upon which he gravely set me down, without a word, & for many days after refused to carry me.

In the window nearest our private entrance my father sat at his table; opposite, at the far end of the library, was another door by which the readers entered.[46] By craning his neck to one side he could see them before they approached his seat; though it was possible by treading very lightly along the Turkey runner, having moreover opened the door with care, as elderly ladies did I noted, to glide up & confront him unexpectedly. One might find him poring over a dictionary or a letter he was writing to his mother or brother, in characters too minute one would think for even his own eyes to decipher, once written. If thus taken by surprise & at a disadvantage, he never showed himself startled or disconcerted, but attended to the reader's wants at a moment's notice like a well[-]oiled automaton. Leaving the library by the visitors' door just mentioned, a wide flight of steps led down to a so-called portico[47] from which you turned on your right into the garden, or on your left down another flight of twelve or fourteen steps into the street.

---

[45] Luisa Hewitt's mother died of a brain haemorrhage in 1885 when Luisa was just four years old. The incident of her death is told in Chapter 3, entitled 'The Earliest Memory' (not included in this edition).

[46] For the location of the librarian's desk and the main entrance see the appendix.

[47] The portico refers to the archway by Room 2, now known as the ceremonial entrance; thanks to Emma Huber for this explanation; the steps lead to St Giles.

Ceremonial entrance via the portico. Photograph Henrike Lähnemann

Or you might go across the archway to our domicile, & the lecture room[48] thereto appended. But the same flight of stairs which led into the portico without, led first into a hall below the library in which were two more lecture rooms: only one of these was of any importance to me, & that was the Duckworth Swann Room.[49]

Busts of Thomas (left) and Robert (right) Finch, now in the Main Reading Room beneath the portrait of Sir Robert Taylor. Photograph Henrike Lähnemann

---

[48] Nowadays the Voltaire Room.
[49] The description that follows seems to refer to what is now known as 'Room 3', the Slavonic Reading Room, which once housed the collection donated by Finch; see David Thomas' blog post on Finch's editions of Giovanni Battista Guarini's *Il Pastor fido*: Bodleian blogs. The other lecture room mentioned here is therefore 'Room 2', which is still in use for lectures.

Here the shelves were filled with English books of the 18th century, & a few rather dreary busts of writers of that age stood about, very much the worse for dust & smoke.[50] This collection was a bequest from the said Swann of whom Papa knew nothing besides to tell me. It must have been a valuable array of early editions [p. 15] they were all calf-bound & beautifully printed, though not so exquisitely as the *Diamond Classics & Aldine Poets of Pickering*[51], a century later, some of which were also scattered up & down these shelves. The room was usually kept locked & rarely visited by anyone, since the books did not strictly serve the purpose of a Modern Language Library such[52] as the Mezzofanti. However there they were, & a great delight to the Few & to me in my later adolescence. In childhood I was chiefly impressed by the busts & a piece of statuary on the fireplace, representing the Dying Gaul[53]. One day an eccentric reader – one of the cranks in whom Fairminster abounded – struck by the resemblance between this figure & my father (which by the way was unmistakeable[54]) delightedly drew his attention to it. Papa hated personal allusions & possibly found a comparison suggesting death particularly distasteful, at any rate, he resented the remark. So he replied rather childishly "And *I* have always thought that it resembled you!" But though this was strictly speaking untrue the fact remains that my father & this oddity bore a certain curious likeness to one another.

---

[50] What is likely meant here are the busts of Robert Finch and his father, Thomas Finch, which are currently on display in the Main Reading Room, positioned in front of the portrait of Sir Robert Taylor above the fireplace. The busts of Voltaire, Diderot and Rousseau, now on display in the Voltaire Room, were a much later addition, acquired in the final quarter of the 20th century. For an overview of the busts in the Taylorian, see the online list of Taylorian Art.

[51] Two 19th-century edition series.

[52] 'like' crossed out before 'such'.

[53] Giles Barber mentions this statue as having been part of the Institution "in days gone by", Giles Barber, 'A Continuing Tradition: Non-Book Materials in the Taylor Institution Library'. In: *Bodleian Library Record* 17.3–4 (2001), pp. 261–267, here p. 263. Unfortunately, this article does not reveal the statue's current location.

[54] 'and he was right' crossed out.

In the Swann Room also hung an oil painting of Ariel on the Bat's Back.[55] It had faded lamentably I suppose for I remember how it came to life for me when it was restored. Someone in authority had agitated & the mist of years had been dispelled. For what to me seemed an infinite age the space on the wall remained empty until one morning Ariel was there again. I said he came to life for me, but I mean it in the material sense. Alas! [H]e was no spirit now; he shone as with varnish, he had grown sleek & lost all his ethereal quality. The silvergreyness he had once shared with the bat, borrowed as it were from the creature's wings, [p. 16] had given way to healthy flesh tints; the plump figure suggested a girl or a girlish boy rather than a fairy, & looked too heavy to be astride of the eerie, less unpleasantly transformed flittermouse. The only pleasing feature was the peacock's feather which in renovated resplendence Ariel waved above his head. But my fancy had been sadly robbed & I was spiritually shocked. Yet I could not avoid the picture. Again & again I returned, hoping against hope to find the spell it had once held ready, the enchantment I still somehow demanded of it. I was conscious of a certain reverence in my father's attitude towards the painting[56] & I sincerely wished to join him in this reverence, yes, even exceed his enthusiasm if that were possible. But all in vain. I still came away from the scrutiny of Ariel with that sense of disillusion that children get on seeing a royal personage for the first time: the king or queen without insignia or a single tuft of ermine; the Prince of Wales in tweeds & a bowler hat. To-day my vision of the Swann Room is more distinct than ever. Once again I seem to sit on the top rung of a safe & comfortable ladder, some fascinating volume in my grasp, devouring it on the spot. Deliberately I recall the mingled smell of dust & old calf & parchment, am conscious of the dusky yellow woodwork, the quills & inkstands & blue writing-paper on the shabbily shrouded tables. Once again I feel the contrast between the din of the traffic outside

---

[55] This painting is now in the Ashmolean Museum, see online list auf artuk.org.
[56] 'painting' typed over another word that is rendered illegible.

& the calm of these countless books, divinely accessible, whose silence I have the power to break at any minute, and by means of this ladder, at any place.

[p. 17] The garden, though public, & practically flowerless, was to me a source of joy. There were twin lawns with steep mounds leading up to the terraces; here I might run & roll by way of exercise, & preparation had I known, for Wykeham Mound College Garden, the favourite school walk some years later. There was the balustrade with its laburnum where I could watch the street & the hotel unnoticed; & there were the four great pillars of the central portico of the Periclean Museum. Round these pillars my mother had played hide & seek with me, & pointed out the pigeons nesting high up in the cornices. We fed them & felt that they were ours. Papa who with all his economies harboured a passion for winged & four[-]footed creatures, bought grain for them every Saturday. On the pediment of the portico the sun-god Apollo sat enthroned, with spikes for rays proceeding from his head. The first time that I saw him from too close a view-point I suffered a severe shock, similar to that which the restored Ariel had produced. It may have been from a porthole in the [n]earest attic, yet I have a vague idea that I managed somehow, somewhere to get on to the leads. Anyhow I found myself nearer Apollo than I ought to have gone or than was good for me. He disillusioned though he did not blind me: for his cheeks were weathered as if blackened by soot, or worse still, swarthy for lack of shaving. He was neither beautiful nor godlike as from below. When I beheld him once more from the usual respectful distance I endeavoured to forget his dirty face. But it took me a long time.

Hand in hand on Sunday afternoons we crossed the garden & entered the Galleries, I tripping along & trying to keep up with Papa's enormous stride. We kept mainly on the ground floor, in the halls of statuary; indeed I have no very early impressions of the pictures & portraits [p. 18] upstairs. I enjoyed the smell of plaster & the coolness like that of a grotto, which seemed to emanate from the statues themselves, as though they were fountains. Greatly awed as in a cathedral or a mausoleum I looked about me. Once Papa led me before the Laokoon & the Niobe, & telling me their myths made considerable cart-wheel tracks in the soft mud of my mind. "But their sons & daughters couldn't help it!" I objected. "The Greek Gods *were* like that," Papa replied, & I acquiesced. After that I would often run backwards & forwards between the two groups, estimating & comparing the extent of their torments. Which suffered most? [O]n the whole I decided in favour of Niobe as the less unfortunate, & would rather have been one of her flock than Laokoon's. I loathed snakes & it must have hurt more to be strangled by these than to be shot with arrows. Silly of them, I thought, to insult their gods; they looked like gods themselves however & gods were apparently unaccountable.

Genius yet ran like blood unspilt upon this battlefield of stone where Time had laid rough hands; but I was too young to see anything except the obvious mutilation. Limbless & headless trunks, down to fragments meaningless save to the artist, met my gaze everywhere, & distressed my sense of harmony. If only they had been whole, if only they could be mended! But people, I soon observed, would not stop to admire or even notice those specimens of sculpture that were complete; & Papa had not much to say about them, to fix my fancy. So that I too in time began to linger before the lady without arms, who could not bless or embrace, & that other lady, with wings indeed, but who could not view or proclaim her triumph. Hoodwinked by chance of centuries they stood or leaned or reclined, a secret society, white & distant, coldly reserving the Past. Dimly, very dimly I surmised that we had been hoodwinked too.

HHHHHHHHHHHHHHHHHHHHHHHHHHHHHHHHHH
XXXXXXXXXXXXXXXXXXXXXXXXXXXXXXXXXX
HHHHHHHHHHHHHHHHHHHHHHHHHHHHHHHHHH

Chapter 37: My Father

[p. 337] My father's virtues might be summed up in one: Rectitude. He was an honest man in the full sense of the word. He was also (like many good people) a very trying man. For his faults were obvious & lay on the surface of his character like weeds & flotsam on the untreacherous canal. It is a paradox that the people we find it easiest to get on with, who are charming, considerate, gracious & conciliatory as companions, have not always on that account the most admirable natures. They may be selfish at heart & too discreet to show it, therefore unselfish in the things that do not matter; deeply suspicious yet apparently confiding; familiar without being friendly disposed; amusing but untruthful; in manner frank but disingenuous in mind; courteous & densely intolerant. Still, what have we to do with the inward man? [I]t is the outward things that touch & trouble us. All that is well concealed is[57] non-existent for practical purposes.[58]

It never occurred to my father that others might be less honest than himself. He trusted everyone implicitly with the exception of German beggars & French Catholics, of whom he had had some exhaustive experience. But lacking imagination he never idealised, so was never disillusioned. He believed, found himself mistaken, & believed again, according to his nature. Himself of a narrow creed, & brought up in a rut of ready-made ideas, he was yet boundlessly tolerant of the creeds & ideas of others[.] Never speculative, his only interest lay in what was verifiable. And here he was chiefly occupied with details, rudiments, & trivialities. [p. 338] Little things delighted, little things annoyed him. Slight contretemps would anger, petty expenses vex, a trifling ailment irritate or depress him. He hated to be contradicted, & any argument provoked him to such a degree that he lost his temper like a child. A child indeed, reserved at heart & with no show of feeling, he was transparent in every other respect. In a dirty world,

---

[57] '(practically)' struck through between 'is' and 'non-existent'.
[58] A handwritten note in the margin reads: 'New Paragraph'. The edition follows this editorial note.

the soul of innocence; in a polite & courtly world, unwelcome, being without the wedding-garment of the graces; in a world of infants & animals entirely at home & beloved.

He was touchy & took offence very easily[59]. Personal remarks, or such as he took to be personal, familiarities or liberties he strongly resented, however well-intentioned & friendly they might be. He preferred to be neglected or ignored. I shall never forget the wrath with which he turned on his landlady at her luncheon table in an Edinburgh boarding-house; she had merely made some pleasantly teasing remark on his misapplied sight-seeing; not wholly uncalled for, since he was recounting at some length his morning's inspection of all the various impossible modern monuments & churches for which the city did not happen to be famous. "But[60] that's not seeing Edinburgh!" she said, "you might as well stay at home" or words to that effect. He was furious, to the embarrassment of myself & the other guests, but especially of poor Miss Mack. To be looked at askance left him indifferent in dog-like dignity, but to be button-holed[61] or teased, exasperated him. This was[62] a species of laziness, of wanting to remain unnoticed, unmolested, owing to the solitary life he had led for many years, before & since my mother's death. Many of his qualities, good as well as bad, but in particular [p. 339] the more trying ones, had probably been aggravated by this circumstance. He possessed a dormant humour, the more attractive for so rarely erupting[63]; but once set going he could laugh over a new story that was related or an old one that he recollected for quite a long time. He would chuckle nervously, almost hysterically, at frequent

---

[59] '(easily took offence)' struck through.

[60] 'you're' struck through following 'But'.

[61] The Oxford English Dictionary defines the verb 'to buttonhole' as '[t]o accost (a person) and detain him or her in conversation as if by taking hold of a buttonhole on his or her clothing', see OED, *buttonhole (v.)*.

[62] 'was' placed in brackets and 'partly' added above – both in pencil.

[63] Alternative wording '(its rare eruptions)' struck through.

intervals, & pull himself up again; discourage my encouragement to proceed, & finally lapse into silence with a self-apologetic air.

From his boyhood my father desired to be trained for the Lutheran ministry. For a time he did study theology at Giessen, & the only story he ever told of that period was how he accompanied his professor to a certain battlefield[64] there, to administer comfort to the dying soldiers. This would be in [].[65] But after preaching his trial sermon, before ordination, he developed throat trouble; & attributing that as the cause, he fancied his voice not strong enough[66] to stand the weekly strain. He changed saddles, (to use the German phrase, "*umsatteln*") & studied philology. It was doubtless a wise course to take, for his voice was not the voice of a preacher, being too highly pitched & consequently sounding strained, even in conversation. It could not have carried far, his sermons would have proved ineffective[67], & this would have mattered considerably in the German Church, where as much[68] importance is attached to the elocution as to the eloquence of the preacher.

So he took his degree of Dr. Phil. at Freiburg i[n] Baden[69] in the year 1868[70], & after a year's tutoring in the family of a [p. 340] Swiss pastor, at Vevey or Montreux, I am not certain which; & having first[,] we may be sure, revisited his mother & sister at D[armstadt][71][,] he came to England in 1870[72]. Here also, he became tutor in the family

---

[64] Specification 'in the district' struck through as Hewitt opted for the shorter version 'there'.

[65] Sentence left incomplete.

[66] Two alternative wordings struck through: 'for the weekly strain (ordeal)'.

[67] Hewitt appears to have been uncertain about the correct adjective at first, but ultimately chose 'ineffective'. '(ineffectual?)' has been struck through.

[68] Alternative wording 'stress is laid' struck through.

[69] Hewitt first typed 'Giessen' as Krebs's place of study, but later corrected it by striking it through and adding 'Freiburg i. Baden' below the line in handwriting.

[70] Only '18' appears in typescript; '68' added at a later point in handwritten ink.

[71] On p. 365f. of the manuscript, Hewitt names Darmstadt as her father's hometown.

[72] As with the previous year mentioned, only '18' typed; '70' added later in handwritten ink.

of the Vicar of Woodhouse Eaves in Leicestershire. It was characteristic of my father that he spoke hardly at all of his experiences at
Montreux, though he often praised the glory of the landscape. He
was not at home with French people, even when they
were Protestants[73]. But of Woodhouse & the Millingtons he talked
freely & frequently. Of the vicar himself, a widower, a kind & genial
country-lover, the gentleman parson of that period; of the two boys
& a friend of theirs who shared their lessons, but chiefly of Edith &
Fanny, the two girls, who won his heart entirely[.] I was to have
been called after Fanny Millington the younger one; but at the last
moment the force of tradition determined my parents on a name already existing in both families. Here on this characteristically English
country-side, in one of the prettiest & compactest villages, my father
must have spent, I think, the happiest year of his life. Even to-day,
motor-ridden, & rudely awakened in more ways than one, Woodhouse Eaves has not lost its original loveliness. [p. 341] The very war-
memorial, rude reminder of a nightmare that will recur unless we
remain wide, wide awake, is a thing of glory to gaze upon. The grey
stone cross stands on a promontory.[74]

At the vicarage my father had his first & only glimpse from within of
English domestic life; he was deeply impressed by its unassuming
homeliness, its uneventful & fussless round. He was also impressed by
the courtesy of the squire who entertained him with frequent hospi-
tality on his estate, presenting him finally with a carved bible containing Raphael drawings, afterwards the delight of my early years.
It was the only time I imagine that he felt & was treated like a member of a family.

---

[73] The latter part of the sentence includes handwritten deletions, indicating that two
syntactic options were originally considered: 'not even with (when they were)
Protestants'.

[74] For a photograph of the war memorial in Woodhouse Eaves see the website of the
Imperial War Museum.

For in the years that followed, at Fairminster, among its exclusive sets he rested ever on the fringe, lonely & awkward, without the power to make himself agreeable to the ladies of the Academic world, & too slow & heavy to mix well with the more brilliant & epigrammatic dons. He could only have mixed with other ponderous pedants; but these like himself awkward & lonely, lacked the social initiative. A very few souls beheld & appreciated the pure child beneath the dowdy tatters of the man. Sometimes he got on quite amazingly well with apparently sophisticated young graduates or undergraduates, & would go walks with them. What they found to talk about Heaven knows, but I gathered from my father's [p. 342] report, that he did most of the talking. His talk was inquisitorial, anecdotal, or concerned with facts: politics or medicine being inevitable in any lengthy conversation. Generally he prefaced his remarks with "Have you heard["] or "Do you know"; "I was present when", "It has been stated" were also very usual phrases with him. When people came to tea, he would take out a small account-book with a glossy black cover, of which he always carried a couple: one for accounts, which he entered with scrupulous accuracy two or three times a day, in[75] infinitesimal hand-writing; the other for memoranda.[76] Nothing was too unimportant to be set down here, from the most trivial daily incidents, to heavy literary & philosophical or theological jottings, excerpts from books he had read, impressions made by these, but never anything personal. He copied whole paragraphs of platitude from volumes not necessarily full of them. He had a veritable flair for truisms & all that was trite. From this [–] in its full sense common-place book [–] he would ladle out information he intended to bestow on

---

[75] 'infinitesimally minute' struck through.
[76] Three of these memoranda books are part of the Taylorian Archives held at the Oxford University Archives under the shelfmark TL 3/27/1–3. For an overview of Taylorian material in the archive's holdings, see the six catalogues listed under 'Taylor Institution' online on the Bodleian's website.

his guest; for it[77] was always one person only[78] whom he would single out remorselessly, like the Ancient Mariner[79] button-holing[80] the wedding-guest; & this one could not choose but hear. "Do you know that if I write to Thomas Cook at his circus[81] (sic) he will supply me with tickets at a reduced rate etc. etc." or "Are you aware that it is now possible to obtain cheap return tickets for the week's end as you do call it?" He would run a phrase or an idiom to death, after hearing it for the first time, misusing or misapplying & generally getting it wrong as in this double instance! "To call a bucket a spade as you do say" was the worst of these howlers.[82] He liked people who were sufficiently amused by his eccentricity to listen patiently while he talked & who would answer his importunate questions to the best of their [p. 343] ability while they quietly studied him. A doctor, a parson, or a student, someone willing to instruct or willing to learn, appealed to his methods most. Of anyone he liked he was almost certain to remark "He is not very strong." or "He appears rather delicate". It was the mysterious mark of his entire approval. Similarly I knew it to be a sign of his affection & solicitude for me, if he observed: "You have a pointed chin again!" meaning that I looked thin & underfed. His unintentionally aggressive tone & manner was not conciliating[83]. Woe to that person for instance who was unable to supply him with

---

[77] To maintain a complete sentence structure, the brackets around 'it' have not been retained in the edition.

[78] '(the willing or unwilling hearer was always one person only)' struck through.

[79] Hewitt here refers to Samuel Coleridge's poem *The Rime of the Ancient Mariner*, first published in 1798 and subsequently revised multiple times. The final version, published in 1834, is available online via the Poetry Foundation.

[80] 'victimising' struck through. For a definition of the verb 'to buttonhole' see fn. 61.

[81] Krebs here refers to Ludgate Circus in London. The renowned travel agency founded by Thomas Cook had its central office at 107–111 Fleet Street, right next to Ludgate Circus.

[82] Krebs's version of the expression – 'to call a bucket a spade' rather than 'to call a spade a spade' – humorously defeats its own purpose: calling things by their true names. Hewitt added this example at a later stage of revision, as it appears in the left margin in handwritten ink.

[83] 'and earned him some life-long enemies' crossed out.

the expected information in his or her own line; he was capable of saying to them: "Then you OUGHT to know!" & making a life-long enemy.

But he was equally irritated when his interlocutor knew too much & replied too fluently where ignorance was expected & would have seemed more fitting. Which brings me to one of his methods – a species of torture he employed. Never having shared as a boy in the obvious cruelties common[84] among other boys, it gave him untold delight to indulge himself now. He would hunt up some remote & uninteresting theme in the Encyclopaedia[85] which he knew to be entirely outside the field of the average scholar; having mastered it more or less, he would submit his partner to a fiery catechism, at the same time supplying the answers & watching his victim's embarrassment: an embarrassment as often as not felt by the latter[86], on his persecutor's account, especially if he happened to see through the device. For with all his artlessness my father could be artful, though again, as a child is artful & cunning. You never knew when he was being really naive, & when he was feigning simplicity.[87]

[p. 344] One day in the library, being extremely busy, or fancying himself so, for he had really very little to do, he met the request of an elderly woman lecturer for a book from one of the topmost shelves, by placing the ladder at a convenient angle for her, with the remark: "You may get it yourself," & leaving her to it. Which being interpreted meant: "I am acutely aware of your honourable position as a graduate of this university; & although you are a female I grant you the extreme privilege of access to books beyond the reach of ordinary

---

[84] 'to (committed by)' struck through; 'among' added in pen above in the line.

[85] 'Brittanica' crossed out.

[86] The original phrase reads 'by the latter as often as not', but a change in syntax is indicated by numbers added in pencil above the words.

[87] An entire sentence struck through: 'In consequence he was not so easy to deal with as might appear'.

readers. Ascend therefore, select, & be thankful!" The intended compliment however was naturally taken as an offence.

At public lectures he was a well-known figure. Stamping, either
much too early or else a little late, into the lecture-room or hall, &
blissfully unconscious of any eyes upon him, he made for the front
row whether reserved or not, & planted himself there with much circumstance of overcoat & umbrella & hat. Then he would spread himself out to his full dimensions with head held slightly forward &
slightly drooping, yawn once, & prepare to listen. "I was present at a
very eloquent oration" or "It was a most instructive lecture" he would
say afterwards; "I could hear every word!"

His umbrellas played an important part in his existence; he possessed
two of them, both of strong alpaca, one a little less shabby than the
other which he used at night.[88] They were both exceedingly large, &
looked as if they had been made to measure. His second-worst nightmare (the worst was missing a train in London & staying the night
at an expensive hotel) was that of [p. 345] losing an umbrella. "I have
had a very bad night" he sometimes informed me at breakfast. "I
dreamt that I left my umbrella in the train, & could not recover it."
He carried it always under his arm; & one day walking behind him
in my eighth or ninth year, I drew his attention to it. "Papa, you're
carrying your umbrella in the wrong way again! I shall be copying
you, & then the girls at school will say, 'Wisa's got that trick from
her father.'" Of this incident I have no recollection but was told by
an aunt who was there at the time; she observed moreover that he
obediently removed the offending object, & carried it in a more normal fashion.[89] So that I did sometimes have a little influence with
him. He nearly always carried an overcoat, of which he also possessed
a couple at different stages of shabbiness. They were of no recognised

---

[88] Various options given in brackets and struck through: '(in the darkness)', '(at
night)' and '(when it was dark)'. The final version, 'at night', added above the line
in handwritten ink.
[89] '(properly)' struck through.

cut, though they approached the clerical[90] in length & colour. "Shall I take my umbrella?"[91] [or] "Is it necessary for me to wear my overcoat, or shall I carry it on my arm?" was the customary appeal to Mrs. Benson or to me before venturing[92] out of doors. It was a risky & regrettable thing to advise him one way or the other; we were to blame if the advice turned out to be wrong; on the other hand it irked him to have it withheld.

He was extremely unwilling to purchase new clothes for himself. His housekeeper had to[93] choose her moments to suggest "Doctor, you need a new suit," or "Doctor, this hat is getting disgraceful, you can't wear it any longer." With luck, if his mood was genial, he would reply "Well then, I must get myself another, & this will do for the evening", & he would frequently follow up such a concession with "At what shop must I buy it?" for he could be as helpless as he could be obstinate[.] [p. 346] Or he would not answer at all, but ruminate on the matter, sometimes for several days, before coming to a decision. If he were feeling disagreeable or not very well, he would snap at Mrs. Benson or me & dispute the fact, or tell us that it was none of our business.

I have said that he was honest; an anecdote of his childhood well shows this trend of character.[94] A great-aunt of mine, who tells me the story,[95] found him one day, standing before the coffee-table, sorely tempted at sight of the sugar thereon. She had entered softly & unobserved, & just in time to see him withdraw his outstretched hand & murmur: "*Nein, [n]ein! [I]ch will kein Stehler sein!*["] (No, no! I will not be a stealer!) Notice his instinctive sense of rhythm: "*Dieb*", the correct word for "thief"[,] would not have sounded half so well.

---

[90] Two words struck through and rendered illegible.
[91] Another word struck through and rendered illegible.
[92] 'forth' struck through.
[93] 'suggest' crossed out.
[94] 'He was discovered by' crossed out.
[95] 'one day before the coffee-table' crossed out.

Still, his honesty did suffer one exception in later life. He thought nothing of defrauding the Railway Companies by making me, when I was ten years old[96] (the then age limit for a half-ticket) sit small in the train. "*Duck Dich!*" (Duck thee!) he would say, just before the guard was expected; I obeyed, but fully conscious of the fraud & the indignity of the situation. On all journeys, & most of all on the voyage to Germany he tried me to the uttermost. The day and a half in the train & on the boat, except while I was asleep or pretending to be, was one continual[97] *embarras des embarras*.

His systematic under-tipping of porters, his unwillingness to procure food in the normal manner of other passengers, the stale sandwiches & repulsive-looking bananas he always carried with him, his way of offering me half of anything he did bring himself to buy, such as a roll or a cup of [B]ovril, offended me in public, & brought the blushes to my face.

[p. 347] But what I hated only a little less than his heated arguments with porters, was the way he would wear one hat over the other in order to save carrying them. A soft clerical hat[98] conspicuously lined and underlined a pseudo-panama of a peculiar shape. Another of his economies which irked me terribly especially on these travels, was that he only shaved once a week. I tried to reason with him that to grow a beard as he used to do in my mother's lifetime & after, would be a yet greater economy, & look much better. But he got so angry that I gave it up[99]. I am ashamed to say that my heart often filled with disgust & loathing as I sat facing him, & observed[100] how he was letting his outer man go to pieces; his vests – he only wore cuffs on rare occasions – showed beneath his coat-sleeves & behind his ill-fitting

---

[96] 'which at that time was' crossed out.
[97] 'embarrassment' struck through.
[98] 'showed' crossed out.
[99] 'at length' struck through.
[100] 'the way he' crossed out.

& protruding front-shirt; his eyes growing blear, with too many pa-
tent medicines I now believe, & his lower lip hanging down uncon-
trolled, & causing an occasional dribble.

This was when he was at his worst; he was able to control himself at
other times. Somehow on travels, or in lodgings, whenever in fact
he felt vague or actual discomfort he became unbearable. Landladies
either loved or loathed him. The good ones made him comfortable,
& therefore found him agreeable; they put up with his constant flow
of questions such as "Can you tell me how far etc." or "In which
direction must I go to etc." or ["]How many inhabitants has
Whitby?["; "]How many[101] lamps in your street?["][102] [Q]uestions
the answer to many of which he might have found in a guide & as
often as not, felt no real concern in knowing. It was just a habit with
him, & his way of making conversation. There were, it is true, one
or two vital questions on his arrival at any new & unknown place; it
was inevitable that he should ask whether the drinking water was
good & not too hard; & where the nearest chemist [p. 348] "resided".
The good landladies were extraordinarily patient with all his whim-
sies, & supplied his many trifling demands for boiled water or baked
apples in & out of season. But the bad landladies would not meet him
an inch, let alone half[-]way; they treated him with suspicion from
the moment they heard his foreign speech & saw his odd ways.[103]
The manner in which he would occupy a small entrance-hall in
shaking his overcoat when he had been in the rain, & opening his
umbrella, leaving it there to dry, – this alone was enough to alienate
the owner of the house, & bring out her sting if she were already
waspish by nature. She sometimes intimated that she was not used to
such lodgers, & remained on the defensive for the rest of our brief
visit. I always felt that I came in for my full share of the disgrace, for

---

[101] 'street' crossed out.

[102] A handwritten note added in the lower margin: 'He actually paced from one end
of our street to the other, (while staying with us,) to ascertain this!'

[103] The following sentence struck through and rendered only partially legible: 'They
were not used to such [?]'.

even[104] towards me this kind of landlady bore a sulky aspect. It was indeed self-revealing when he remarked how often servants &[105] servers behind counters would declare "We are not used to such a request" though I suspect they said "We are not usually asked for such an article"[;] even in shops he delighted to disconcert the manager[106] whose presence he habitually demanded when he lodged some petty complaint about mouldy marmalade or goods that had risen by a halfpenny since the previous week.[107]

I have said that my father was a slave to routine. For over 40 years he went through the same daily programme with very few variations, enough to prove the rule (of monotony). Here is a typical day in detail as accurate as I am able to supply.

His housekeeper would ascend the three flights of stairs to his bedroom & knock him up with some hot water & [p. 349] tea at 7.30. Having donned [his] canvas carpet slippers & his grey camel's hair dressing-gown (renewed only once within my memory) he first went across the landing into the library; here he examined the morning letters left by the porter on his desk[108]; then he came down as far as the first landing & entered the sittingroom, where he sat down to the piano & played one or two verses of a hymn, followed by a tune from the operas; of these he had a selection of easy settings, in a bound volume surviving from his boyhood. A few chosen hymns recurred with frequency. "When I survey" was his actual favourite, & he sang it with unction & out of tune in church. Another was "Abide with me" because my mother had loved it. "Sun of my Soul"

---

[104] 'with' crossed out.

[105] Two words crossed out with only the first remaining legible 'people'.

[106] 'whom he' crossed out.

[107] 'To return to the [?] landladies.' crossed out.

[108] 'writing table' crossed out.

he played for the same reason, but more often on a Sunday even-ing[.][109] Once he took exception to the word "Experience" in a hymn, as being unpoetical, & substituted another in its stead. I forget what it was, but a cliché certainly & no improvement. After five minutes of[110] hymn-playing my father opened the window & looked at the thermometer hung there by his own hands, then he descended to the basement & the "Big Room" where he rang the bell. At the summons Mrs. Wren[-Bootle] or Mrs. Benson brought in the hot water for his sit-bath as he called the old-fashioned hip-bath which served our common[111] turn. He washed himself with scrupulous & pedantic precision, for cleanliness came next to godliness with him. The Mezzofanti, as so many even younger buildings in those days, lacked the conveniences of a bathroom, as also of indoor sanitation;[112] though during my time the latter was installed for the porter! [M]y father might no doubt have[113] demanded an equal consideration, but it was his practise never to ask for anything [p. 350] that would cost money if he could avoid it. Having finished his matutinal ablutions which took some considerable time, he dressed & rang again for the débris of the bath to be removed, & breakfast brought in. In the latter years he persuaded his housekeeper, Mrs. Benson, to pedicure him two or three times a week; or else it was she who persuaded him to accept her services in this capacity; I cannot be certain which, but only that it was an amicable arrangement to which Mrs. B[enson] did not object. She & her predecessor both referred to "the Doctor" as "a just man" in spite of their admission that he tried them exces-sively. They were always willing to do his extra biddings, thereby[114] spoiling him & making him more insufferable.

---

[109] The Christian hymns mentioned here are *Abide with Me* (1847) by Henry Francis Lyte, *When I Survey the Wondrous Cross* (1707) by Isaac Watts and *Sun of my Soul, Thou Saviour Dear* (1820) by John Keble.

[110] 'this relaxation' struck through.

[111] 'need(s)' struck through and 'turn' added in handwriting above the line.

[112] 'a point I have touched on in an early chapter;' struck through.

[113] 'insisted on the same' crossed out.

[114] 'of course downright' struck through.

At breakfast, if I happened to be at home,[115] he would talk a little if agreeably disposed or, as happened more frequently, complain a great deal about his general & particular ill-health, & the bad night he had sustained, as also about the indifferent breakfast[.][116] When he had rung for the clearing of the table & Mrs. Benson entered he would continue his remarks about the badness of her cooking. Sometimes she took it in good part or made some feeble protest about the way he kept the food waiting, at other times she ignored his grumblings. When he showed continuous irritability she gave him notice & he grew affable again. "Doctor, I shall have to leave you; I can't do anything right it seems." "Well, Mrs. Benson, I am sorry if I spoke hastily," & things went on as before. In her [p. 351] cooking Mrs. Benson lacked imagination, & though my father had laid down a weekly menu from the beginning, to ensure digestible dishes & avoid unwelcome surprises & unfamiliar fare, he would have been secretly relieved I think to have had the monotony of his régime broken in a reasonable way[117]. Grounds for dissatisfaction were abundant, though often enough he passed over such crimes as watery potatoes[,] greasy soup, over-baked puddings, & complained of trifling omissions that were easily remedied; as for example "skin*less* hot milk" or a blunt knife.

While the table was being cleared he vanished behind a curtain to clean his teeth. Once there had been no curtain. I had a serious struggle with him over this, & later on, over the arrangement of the rooms in general. A little further along the passage towards the kitchen was a tiny room, a den indeed, called the beer-room, as already elsewhere

---

[115] A longer passage struck through: 'I came in from the inner room which was my bedroom, & which had no separate entrance, until later when I preferred an attic, 124 steps higher. During this meal'.

[116] A further substantial portion of text struck through: ', this last complaint embarrassed me in as much as it was justified, & I was in no position to do anything about it except agree'.

[117] 'reasonably broken' crossed out.

indicated[118]. It was called so for no better reason than that three successive servants had stored their beer there, in the form of a barrel that[119] was renewed every three weeks with unfailing regularity. Nothing else occupied the room save spiders & the outlook was on to a blank wall. A suggestion that Papa should turn this place into a dressing-room which was about all it was fit for, met with no success, though the solution was obvious; but when years afterward I turned it, with the minimum of expense & trouble, into a dining-room, as being moreover a little nearer the kitchen, I failed[120] to carry through my plan. Only once was he persuaded to have a meal there, which ended, on his part in anger, & in tears on mine. He was too much the creature of habit to break one, however bad it might be. On any other point he could be tractable, & brought to reason, but you could not [p. 352] persuade him to break an old custom. So he returned to his washstand corner in the "Big Room" & all that I was able to effect was the screening of it off by[121] the aforesaid curtain. I well recollect the tedious trouble Mrs. Benson & myself had in extracting the money from him for this.

In the winter my father would take his cod liver oil immediately after his breakfast, & then glance at his "*Wand-[K]alendar*". This was from a German magazine of extreme Protestant tone, called after Gustaf Adolf,[122] whom I had reason to detest, having heard too much about

---

[118] For the first reference of this room, see the respective passage in Chapter 1 (p. 4 in the manuscript).

[119] 'stood on two trestles &' struck through.

[120] 'lamentably' crossed out.

[121] 'a curtain' struck through.

[122] Hewitt here refers to the magazine published by the Gustav-Adolf-Werk, the Protestant Church of Germany's association for supporting its work abroad. The organisation was founded in the 19th century and named after the Swedish king Gustav II Adolph (1594–1632), whose military intervention was of key importance to the Protestant cause in the Thirty Years' War, see the website of the Gustav-Adolf-Werk.

him. My uncle in Darmstadt had instructions to send us the aggressive rag each month. On the calendar my father made minute entries about the weather & memoranda for hair-cut etc.

Then Mrs. Benson having mentioned any article of grocery she had forgotten or was out of, or one which he preferred to get himself, he set out for his morning constitutional. It was almost invariably down the Rye Mart, around Gabriel[123] Fields & back through Ilex Alley & Tweeny Lane[124], or Lemon St., if he had to interview the Binder Mr. Page.[125] Or if he wanted to pick up some parcel at Gander & Soars'[126][,] the grocers, he would go by Tweeny Lane & come back by the Rye. Sometimes,[127] he chose to go round the Chase & the Herboretum by way of a change; he would combine this with a visit to the Chase Museum or the Urania, where he insisted[128] on seeing the Keeper or the Professor on some trifling business.[129] On the homeward way he frequently looked in on Bros.[130] Pryce &

---

[123] 'Gabriel' typed above a crossed-out word, which is now illegible.

[124] While 'Tweeny Lane' is not part of Simmons's list of pseudonyms, it may – judging from the context given here – refer to Turl Street as Hewitt describes it as part of a walk back into town from Christ Church Meadows, having already renamed Magpie Lane as 'Ilex Alley'. It cannot be High Street as the pseudonym for High Street is 'Great Orange Street'.

[125] 'Unless he had' crossed out.

[126] This shop name is not included in Simmons's list of pseudonyms.

[127] 'his one alternative' crossed out.

[128] 'he saw the (insisted)' struck through; 'he insisted' added in handwriting above the line.

[129] The list of pseudonyms identifies 'The Chase' as 'The Parks', that is the University Parks, so 'Chase Museum' could refer to the Museum of Natural History (which included the Pitt Rivers Museum at the end of the 19th century). The anthropologist Edward Burnett Tylor served as Keeper of the Museum from 1883 to 1909; see the relevant entry in the online database Oxford Dictionary of National Biography. Emma Huber pointed out that 'Herboretum' could refer to the University Parks Nursery and 'Urania' to the University Observatory, see a contemporary map.

[130] One word crossed out, most likely 'Williams'.

Pritchard[131] to renew a prescription or buy some cheap new drug recommended by anybody. A [G]erman doctor once said to[132] him, hearing of all his pills & doses: "Why, you're the veriest medicine chest!" He took everything supposed good for any particular malady, whether he had that [p. 353] malady or not. For instance, black currant jam being voted good for the throat, it became a permanent addition to[133] his table.

He carried a black Gladstone bag, very shiny & shabby in appearance, when he had no umbrella. In this bag he brought back the commodities from his grocer or wine-merchant. "Shall we send them for you, Sir?" was invariably met with "No, I thank you, I will take them myself." For one thing he feared the goods might not arrive in time, or not be the one he had specified; & for another thing he felt it was not befitting an ordinary citizen to have his food sent him if he was able to carry it. The nobility no doubt ordered their groceries just as they kept their carriages, but he, a burgher (as he would have described himself) had nothing to do with them.

The library opened at eleven, & at eleven precisely the librarian was found in situ. In later years however it was oftener five minutes past than five minutes before the actual hour that he appeared. To this much of slackness he had succumbed. But in Fairminster slackness was an admitted & time-honoured quality to which my father merely in the end conformed. His burden was an easy one. True, the library was haunted by a few exigent bores whose garrulity there was out of place: the sort of readers who having no right & no scheme cause more trouble than the legitimate student. There was Dr.[134] Lloyd-Lloyd who monopolised the sunniest window & discussed winter- & summer underwear, a subject Papa found irresistible, in loud tones,

---

[131] '(the chemists)' struck through. This shop is included in Simmons's list of pseudonyms.
[132] 'told' crossed out; 'said to' typed above the line.
[133] '(on)' struck through.
[134] Hewitt originally typed 'Mr.', but corrected it to 'Dr.' by hand.

to the horror of maiden ladies, who were there to read their French shockers in peace, under the pretext of keeping up their knowledge of the language; & there was Mr. Bloggs or Plox as Papa called him, who wore a velvet jacket & ran round the library with his hands in his pockets, whistling. Of him my father mildly complained to the Guardians as in duty bound, he opined; but they merely [p. 354] supplied him with an anecdote for his slender collection, to be trotted out on sundry future occasions; "leave him alone!" they said, "he is a genius!" At which my father marvelled greatly. And there was Major Campbell who wore black knee-breeches & a long black beard, & lived alone, letting down a basket for his bread from an upper window sooner than interview his baker. He did his own housework too, & took tremendous strides in the street, & never looked at a woman. He would talk to my father by the hour. I suspect that his politics were as unsound as his social economy, & that he harboured some half-baked religion. But apart from these inevitable cranks, to be found in every reading-room, Papa had a light task. He catalogued a few new books & periodicals that had been bought in the previous week; submitted others on approval to the bench in the Guardians' Room, to be inspected[135] by them at the weekly Saturday meeting; set aside books for the binder, & replaced those returned thence, on the shelves; trotting, or rather tramping up & down the ladders with a will, as though he relished this form of exercise & thought it good for him, which no doubt it was. From his desk in one of the windowed recesses, the furthest from the main entrance, he was yet able to observe any that entered by craning his neck round the corner. Through his window he looked out on the front of the Periclean[136], crowned by the weathered Apollo: that pillared facade[137]

---

[135] Initially, Hewitt typed 'viewed (reviewed?)', but crossed both options out and added 'inspected' above the line by hand.

[136] 'Periclean' added in handwritten ink above a typed word that has been crossed out and is now illegible.

[137] Hewitt first typed two options 'stately facade (pillared facade)', but struck through the former.

to which the wheeling pigeons gave perpetual breath[138]. For these stray birds my father with incongruous extravagance bought a weekly allowance of grain, thus enticing them to stay & haunt the sills & ledges[.][139] From the windows on the far side of my father's corner, he gained a view of St. Joseph's College & [p. 355] part of Nimrod College; the Pretender's Pillar also, half hidden by elms could just be seen. Rarely more than one or two readers occupied the library at the same time; the less than dozen chairs nearly always stood empty. Sometimes a luxurious reader would draw up one to the enormous[140] fireplace & here relapse into a half-roasted condition of coma; I did myself on occasion. As a rule the librarian had the floor to himself, & at his table might poddle with minutiae to his heart's content, or potter with a new language or dialect. Fortunately for him his hobby & his job were one & the same; of one[141] tongue after another did he patiently plod through the elements until he had mastered them. I believe he was the only man in Europe who had ever been able to transcribe Sarmatian.[142] Only once, & that in his youth, he allowed his imagination to range beyond "book-learning", & for a brief space cherished the desire of becoming a carpenter; but this interest was doomed to remain academic.

At half past twelve he would disappear through the door behind his chair & run downstairs, to drink according to his medical adviser's direction a glass of boiled water, of which a jug was always kept filled & stood[143] in the niche by his washstand. He sipped it gradually, standing on tip-toe between the sips, to emphasise the intervals as it were. After this he again ran upstairs, two steps at a time; first peeping

---

[138] '(lent a fluttering breath) & intermittent defilement' struck through.

[139] 'with intermittent defilement.' struck through.

[140] At least two words have struck through and thereby been rendered illegible.

[141] 'language' crossed out.

[142] The Sarmatian people were a people of Iranian origin 'who migrated from Central Asia to the Ural Mountains between the 6th and 4th century BC and eventually settled in most of southern European Russia and the eastern Balkans'; see Encyclopedia Britannica, *Sarmatian*.

[143] '(&standing)' crossed out.

through the little curtain of dusty & shabby green taffeta that was drawn across the glass in the door (everything at the Mezzofanti was dusty & shabby) – to discover if anyone had arrived in his absence; unreasonably I used to think, for it merely delayed him a shade longer. But he did not like surprises. He entered, only to emerge once more at 1 o'clock, when his domestic [help][144] [p. 356] toiled up the stairs with his dinner-tray. Here in the grey stone[145] landing at a small inkstained table defaced by caricatures, once perpetrated[146] by[147] students at lectures & exams[,] he rapidly consumed a stand-up[148] lunch; darting backwards & forwards between the table & the door, to peep through the[149] gap in the curtain, which, what with him[150] & myself & the housekeeper all pulling at it, was wearing into shreds that threatened to become visible from the other side. Between the courses of[151] his meal he was back at his desk; till again the breathless attendant knocked, with his milk-pudding & prunes or stewed apples. One wonders whether in the thirty & odd years during which three successive housekeepers presided over his kitchen he never wearied of the weekly menu he had drawn up once for all; which never varied except in the holidays; & whether it was not a relief on these occasions to get away from it, even to the indifferent – but at least different – fare of a second-rate landlady.

---

[144] The word 'help' has, in fact, been struck through but is retained in this edition for syntactic clarity. Following 'help', the phrase 'Mrs. Benson or whoever it might be at the time' has likewise been struck through.

[145] 'lobby' crossed out.

[146] 'having been used' struck through; 'perpetrated' added above the line by hand.

[147] 'some' added above the line by hand, but subsequently struck through.

[148] 'Standing', as originally typed, amended to 'stand-up' in handwritten ink.

[149] 'foresaid' crossed out.

[150] Hewitt originally typed 'me' instead of 'him', but crossed it out to give her father precedence – presumably because naming oneself first was and still is considered impolite.

[151] 'Between the courses of' added in typescript below a crossed-out 'At intervals between'.

SUNDAYS. Bone Soup, Roast Joint, Baked Potatoes & Greens (the latter of course varying in their seasons, they couldn't help it!) Yorkshire Pudding, if Mrs. W[ren-Bootle] or B[enson] had time & was[152] well disposed.

MONDAYS. Same Soup. Mince, Boiled Potatoes & Carrots or Turnips.

TUESDAYS. Similar Soup, Rissoles, Mashed Potatoes & other veg[etables] in season.

WEDNESDAY. Similar Soup. Cold remains of Joint, Boiled or Mashed Potatoes[.]

THURSDAY. Similar Soup, thicker. Roast Chicken tasting boiled. Baked Potatoes & other veg[etables] usually cauliflower.

FRIDAY. Similar Soup, thinner. Fish, (nearly always Plaice;[153] by courtesy described as Sole on the weekly account[)].

SATURDAY. No soup. Cold Chicken Bits, with cold pork or bacon, [p. 357] this last not in the bond but afterwards to become the cornerstone of the housekeeper's nightly meal.

No pudding on Wednesdays or Saturdays, but sausages for Wednesday's supper & Omelette or hardbaked macaroni cheese for Saturday's; on other nights the supper consisted of Cocoa or Bovril & the remains of the midday milk-pudding, followed by an infinitesimal fraction of cheese & biscuits, more often than not accompanied by the reflection that "cheese digests everything except itself."

---

[152] The alternative 'felt' struck through.
[153] 'though' crossed out and 'by courtesy' added above the line.

Such[154] was the unmodified Bill of Fare[155] throughout the year. Only that[156] in summer a revolting salad of mashed potatoes dyed with beetroot replaced the Wednesday & Saturday vegetables. I think this salad like one or two other items was owing to an initial mistake or misunderstanding, which had never been rectified. It was handed down orally by Sarah to Mrs. Wren-Bootle & by her to Mrs. Benson.

At 5 p.m. the library closed to the public but my father still found plenty wherewith to occupy himself[157] for another half-hour before leaving. Then he walked round the[158] Chase & Herboretum, except on summer Thursdays, when he made a point of getting off at 4.45, persuading the porter to[159] occupy his seat in the library for the last 15 minutes. He was thus enabled to go further afield, either to Muchett, Sageby, Lambcote or along the dust-ridden & dreary Bugley Rd. & through the derelict village of Mouseaton, up the corn-covered hills to Hedghogston.[160] Out in the fields he would sit on a stile to rest & eat some fruit,[161] & perhaps enter some memoranda into his note-book; then wending slowly home, he [p. 358] reached the Mezzofanti by eight o'clock, in time to fetch his supper from the kitchen stove, as Thursday was one of Mrs. Benson's nights[162] out. He found his pudding usually baked beyond recognition, a withered heap, crusted & chipped throughout; his cocoa also crusted with skin

---

[154] The sentence originally started with 'In the latter years', but this phrase has been crossed out.

[155] 'Bill of Fare' added above 'programme' which has in turn been crossed out.

[156] The text first reads 'Except that', but Hewitt crossed it out and typed the stylistic variation 'Only that' above the line.

[157] 'before leaving to the' crossed out.

[158] 'University' struck through.

[159] 'take his place' struck through.

[160] Sageby and Mouseaton are the only two of the villages mentioned here that Simmons included in the list of pseudonyms: he equated 'Sageby' with Cumnor and 'Mouseaton' with Hinksey. Emma Huber identified 'Lambcote' as possibly a punning reference to Wolvercote (lamb/wolf), 'Bugley Road' as Botley Road and 'Hedghogston' as possibly Boar's Hill.

[161] 'then he returned home' crossed out.

[162] Hewitt typed 'off (out)', but handwritten corrections give preference to 'out'.

half an inch thick, standing in a saucepan of hot water on the hob, for the last two hours or so. I gathered that he preferred it so, imagining the crust to be nutritious & possess the value of cream; it looked a revolting mess, & was made still less attractive by the cup which contained it; for this cup through constantly dwelling in simmering water, had become charred & so reticulated with cracks as almost to form a design. If I was at home & did not happen to accompany him on his long walk, I sat in the kitchen, always glad to have the opportunity of the housekeeper's absence, or to sit there with her when she invited me & was expecting no visitors; for it was the one cosy spot in the building[163] except the porter's[164] dwelling — I presume.[165] Whether I went or stayed however, I brought in the supper[166] on these Thursdays, after I was about twelve[167] years old. Later I used to long to make his cocoa freshly at the last minute, but never dared suggest to Mrs. Benson that she should leave it to me. And when I asked Papa to tell her, either he didn't dare, or, as I said, he really liked his overcooked victuals in spite of their appearance.

After his evening meal, of which he generally partook in[168] his dressing-gown[169] he cleared the things away & carried the tray out into the kitchen, when Mrs. Benson was not there to answer the bell. After that he drew the leather armchair a little nearer – not too near – the fire, so that his feet could [p. 359] rest on the leather couch, & the

---

[163] 'besides' struck through.

[164] Hewitt originally typed 'kitchen (dwelling)', but the former as well as the brackets have been struck through.

[165] Brackets around the final 'd' of 'presumed' crossed out.

[166] Hewitt typed 'his supper' first, but crossed it out and went for 'the supper'.

[167] 'nine' crossed out, 'twelve' added above the line.

[168] 'a' struck through and 'his' added in handwritten ink above the line.

[169] The typescript originally continued with 'the grey camel's hair one already mentioned', but this specification has been struck through by hand. The gown is indeed mentioned on p. 349 of the typescript.

table with the light[170] was behind him.[171] My father now settled down to study a few verses of the New Testament in some one of the imperfectly understood languages of his choice. Then he would read aloud to me, some light book of memoirs or a German classic, anything but a modern[172] work of fiction. In his last years he enjoyed [George] Borrow & [Thomas] Hardy & Jane Austen, & read me these, also [Charles] Dickens & [T]*he Vicar of Wakefield* [by Oliver Goldsmith], but never more than one chapter a night. He refused to undertake any book however much recommended that had long chapters, or worse still, none at all.[173] He was easily tickled by what he read aloud, & punctuated every amusing paragraph with chuckles.

In sitting thus, he would sometimes allow "the Cat" to get upon his knee. We had a grey tabby called "Cairo" & before that a black one, Olga,[174] who was a loose piece & had to be destroyed. (She developed nympholepsy.) Cairo was a respectable eunuch with no imagination. Papa[175] considered it indecent to refer to the sex of an animal or to give them personal names. Every cat was "[s]he", & otherwise "the Cat". If you must address[176] her[177] & there was no reason why you should[178], except with a mute gesture of the hand, you called her[179] "Puss", & *that* was a concession. I am reminded here that even to me he never alluded by my Christian name; whether in this case he felt

---

[170] 'above it were' stuck through.

[171] A whole sentence that originally followed crossed out: 'At one time of course it was a lamp which stood on the table, afterwards giving place to gas, & this in turn to electric light.'

[172] 'story' crossed out.

[173] A whole sentence crossed out: 'This was unpardonable & shocked him.'

[174] The sentence originally ended after 'Olga' and a new sentence started with 'The latter', but corrections in handwritten ink were added that account for the syntactic structure given above.

[175] 'thought' crossed out.

[176] An alternative to 'address' given below the line and crossed out: 'apostrophise'.

[177] Hewitt here corrected 'it' to 'her', in keeping with her father's habit of addressing cats in the feminine.

[178] 'do so' crossed out.

[179] 'might call it' corrected to 'called her'.

it too intimate or too undignified, I cannot say: but I was always referred to as "his daughter". So Cairo in succession to Olga jumped, after due deliberation, on to his lap & kneaded the [p. 360] camel's hair dressing-gown. "Well, she may cure my sciatic pain," he would say, almost apologetically, as the creature spread its full length along his thigh. And sometimes he would place her behind his back or across his shoulders, hoping that the electricity in her body might communicate itself beneficially to him.

After urging me at intervals to go to bed, he would, when I at last obeyed, between ten & eleven o'clock, himself in a leisurely way undress by the fire, putting away books at intervals & talking to himself, enumerating most of his actions with "*Eins. Zwei. Drei. So. Nun kommt das.*" (One. Two. Three. There. Now comes that.) & yawning very audibly. I used to hear all this through the door, & how he slowly ascended the stairs to his bedroom. His[180] footsteps[181] on the echoing stone were followed by the sound of a reverberating door upstairs. It was generally the signal for me[182] to get out of bed & back to the fire, which latterly I had the courage to mend, relighting the lamp, & settling down to a book in the same way in which I had seen Papa do. I put my feet up on the sofa, & only deplored that "the Cat" had been mercilessly relegated to the kitchen or the area, whence I dared not fetch her again. Sometimes I helped myself to biscuits or bread & marmalade or jam from the cupboard, by way of fillip to my studies; studies which needless to say were concerned with fairy-tales, poetry, & infantile belles-lettres, none of them in the least serious.

Thus ended my father's day. The Sunday he divided to a certain extent from the week. He rose half an hour later & attended the University Sermon at S[t]. Mark's[183] where he listened attentively, in his

---

[180] 'His' originally preceded by the word 'generally', which has been crossed out.

[181] 'dying' crossed out.

[182] The original read 'the signal for me generally', but a change in syntactic structure is indicated by numbers typed below the line.

[183] Simmons did not include St. Mark's in his list of pseudonyms, yet this term must refer to the University Church of St Mary the Virgin on High Street in Oxford.

favourite attitude with head bent forward; subsequently bestowing liberal [p. 361] praises on the preacher when the latter was audible. On the way home he regularly called in at[184] the [c]hemist[']s, (a.) because drugs were to him a daily necessity & delight, & (b.) because the shop was open. He encouraged any business that happened to be open on Sundays or after hours, unless it were for the sale of sweets or tobacco! At the chemist's he produced an empty bottle either for the halfpenny or for a refill; then he bombarded Mr. Pryce with questions on Welsh philology which that gentleman was not prepared to answer, & Mr. Pritchard with questions on articles[185] displayed upon the counter which he himself was not prepared to purchase. And to the pair of them he offered solutions of political problems, which they were not prepared to accept & which must often have shocked them to the marrow. After his midday meal, a late & a long one, drawn out by an orange & sometimes – very rarely – a port-wine glass full of Burgundy, for he was abstemious without being a full-time tea-totaller, he would wander across to S[t]. Joseph's Garden[186] to admire the rockery, & go up Little Mound Arimathea (which alas! no longer exists). I always accompanied him on this jaunt if I was at home; & I liked going up the mound, on the top of which there was a seat, & a view of other gardens. He made a rule of circumambulating S[t]. Joseph's garden three times, – or sometimes four, saying "Four for a girl", because I was with him. Sometimes we went out to tea, with Professor Hans Halle, or Professor Baker Watts[187], – or some retired don or dignitary of the Church, usually a bachelor, in some country house on the outskirts of Fairminster, in Rueville, Muchett,

---

[184] The chemist's name 'Pryce & Pritchard' crossed out; see Simmons's list of pseudonyms.

[185] 'adorning the counter' struck through.

[186] As the list of pseudonyms renders 'St Joseph's Street' as 'St John's Street', Emma Huber suggests that the garden referred to here is most likely Wellington Square.

[187] The following phrase 'whose little son reminded me of Little Lord Fauntleroy' and a few now illegible words struck through. In the list of pseudonyms compiled by Simmons, Professor Baker Watts is rendered as 'Professor Baker White'.

or on [p. 362] Lavenstock Hill.[188] No particulars of these excursions occur to me, except that my father talked very much &, ate very little; [h]e often poured his tea into his saucer; neither greedy nor epicurean, if he took a lustful pleasure in anything it was in pills & medicine.

A word remains to be said of his habits in regard to drinking & smoking.[189] He would make a bottle of Mosel or Claret last him for weeks, by drinking one small glass on Sundays; & then he would sometimes make an interval in which he took no wine at all. He also took with fair regularity half a pint of lager beer with his supper, but only twice a week; & if he were out of it, he might perhaps, but this was rare, condescend to ask his housekeeper for a glass from her barrel. As for smoking, he almost barred it, as being bad for the throat. Once a year he was liable to have one of the cigars which he had smuggled over from Germany in twos or threes, year by year; & of which his collection was somewhat antique. If one was offered him, he carefully wrapped it up, & put it in his pocket to add to his store; & when he offered one he would detach it with his fingers from the case & hand it over with a gingerly & almost reverend care.

A few more characteristic anecdotes about my father I will set down here by way of postscriptum.

He once told me of a practical joke he permitted himself to play quite seriously upon the management of a London Hotel. He told them he was travelling round on a tour of inspection, with a view to reporting on English Hotels & their system! The result of this ruse was that he met with the promptest attention & extreme deference, which was what he intended.[190] [p. 363]

---

[188] 'Rueville' is identified as 'Summertown', 'Muchett' and 'Lavenstock Hill' not.
[189] The following phrase ', which as I have said, were most abstemious' struck through.
[190] 'of course' struck through.

One of the readers of[191] the Mezzofanti died, having previously borrowed a number of books from the library. As the volumes were not immediately returned, my father, never having heard of the term "executor", addressed the following communication[192] to "The Late C. N. Esq."[193]: "Sir, since you can no longer have any possible use for the copy of ..., please to return it at once to the library!".[194]

As an instance of his elementary & superficial selfishness, I should recount an incident of his later life, when he was staying with me after my marriage. It was an August Bank Holiday & after lunch we took him into the city, to show him the few sights of which it boasted. His avidity in this respect was boundless, including every church & chapel & monument, however hideous or unimportant. Having at length exhausted the objects of his interest as well as ourselves[s] we looked about us for a café or restaurant where we might restore our jaded spirits with tea. But every blind was drawn & every door was shuttered in the intolerably forbidding manner they assume on this secular Sabbath of the[195] nation. Weary with wandering & more than weary[196] of the function of guides we uttered some mild complaints & protests; but they were met with the sublimely innocent reflection: "Well, it is a fortunate[197] thing that I have had my coffee." Unfortunately we had not. Being in haste, we had barely had time to give him his.

However, to balance this story which illustrates what I called a superficial selfishness, it is only right to prove that it did not go deep;[198]

---

[191] Hewitt typed 'in' above 'of' but did not cross 'of' out.
[192] 'the following communication' has been added above the line by hand; the original remains only partly legible as it has been crossed out: '& printed [?]-card'.
[193] The reader's name struck through and rendered illegible apart from 'C.' and 'Esq.'. The initial 'N.' added above the line by hand.
[194] The exact wording of the note has been added between the lines by hand.
[195] '(British)' struck through.
[196] 'with (being questioned)' struck through.
[197] Hewitt typed 'good' first, but crossed it out and added 'fortunate' below the line.
[198] 'by showing' crossed out.

my father only stayed a week with us, yet insisted before he left, that we should accept the same sum that he would have paid[199] in the most exorbitant lodgings. [p. 364] Our protests were met with the after all just rejoinder that we were not affluent, & that he would have spent his holiday in lodgings had he not spent them with us.

I have alluded to his country walks & his fondness for animals. Before setting out, especially in the holidays when he had unlimited leisure, he would collect scraps of bread & stale biscuits in crumpled paper bags that had served the same purpose many times already. His pockets always crunched with paper bags containing crumbs. At every farm he passed, he would stop, & if there were fowls in sight as there usually were, he would feed them from these supplies, being very careful to distribute fairly & equally among them, so that each chicken obtained a portion, if only the minutest. This became such a regular habit, that it was apt to cause inconvenient delays, in particular, during one summer holiday on Dartmoor, where two cousins had joined us who disliked such delays. Papa inquiring of them one morning how many hours a certain walk we contemplated would take to accomplish, one of the cousins promptly replied, "Plus chickens, 3½ hours, minus chickens, 2½."[200]

Similar was the manner in which on Sundays he regaled the deer at Coverley's College with chestnuts he assiduously collected all through the week. He had a peculiar low & drawn-out whistle with which he coaxed those creatures to the gate at which he stood. They knew it & responded by coming towards him at their stately leisure from any distance in the Park where they were herded. He took a childish joy in rustling his paper bag & in producing & distributing

---

[199] 'for board & lodging' crossed out.
[200] The following passage starting with 'Similar was the manner' and ending with 'barn-doors & farmyards' is added on a smaller slip of paper that has been attached to p. 364 and labelled 'p. 364' as well. The precise location for its insertion is indicated on the original p. 364 by hand.

the nuts with the same scrupulous equity he employed outside the barn-doors & farmyards.

In company a singular effect was frequently produced by his retailing news freshly gathered from a foreign weekly & already stale in this country; items of information concerning British Affairs & those of the Empire which had passed through a continental limbeck[201] & were duly coloured thereby.

Though he disliked strong tea, he disapproved as strongly of water being added on the table, either to the pot, or, still more unpardonably, to his cup. The[202] mysterious process of tea-making, he [p. 365] chose to delude himself should have been completed[203] in the kitchen where it was begun.

By some official oversight he exercised a political vote for a number of years; but once before a General Election he received the following communication from headquarters: "You have been deprived of your vote as an unnaturalized alien." At this he took deep offence. I remember, – it was in my holidays – how he ran downstairs from the library & communicated the indignity as he conceived it[204] to my unintelligent & wholly unsympathetic ears! Perhaps the phrase does appear to contain something accusatory[205]; it seemed to him possibly to combine a moral reflection (that of unnatural vice) with an insult – the doubt of his sanity.

I have forgotten to mention his favourite occupation which was visiting the Sick, to register symptoms & ailments, comparing them

---

[201] Figurative use of limbeck, that is 'alembic', which the Oxford English Dictionary defines as 'An early apparatus used for distilling', see OED *limbeck (n.)*.
[202] 'mystery' struck through.
[203] This sentence was originally typed in a way that allowed for different wordings: 'should be (have been) completed (accomplished)', but emendations by hand suggest the version given in the edition.
[204] 'to be' struck through.
[205] '(of an accusation)' struck through.

with his own; visiting doctors was also a great treat. Of these he never consulted less than two or three at a time, & at the end of every consultation he would draw out his purse with a slightly tremulous hand & the question: "What have I to pay?"

Hardly ever did he strike a match but used paper spills which he was always making; this was characteristic of his economy. And when he found a hole in his socks he inserted one of these spills, & laid the article on the sopha to attract the attention of his housekeeper or myself. When I announced my intention of getting married his first objection after the obvious one that I should have enough to live on without such an expedient, was: "But who will mend my socks?" And as a last resort "You can have him for a friend as much as you like!" was of course wholly innocent of implication![206]

He died shortly after the Great Peace, at Darmstadt, in a [p. 366] Franciscan Hospital; his[207] desire, that of retiring to his native town having been granted him, but for how brief an interval; he only drew one quarter's pension. The Brother who nursed him, as devotedly as a Franciscan Brother would, & was with him to the last, night & day, told me about their frequent talks together. Of my father's undisguised Evangelical convictions & his great respect at the same time for his Catholic entourage & for Catholics individually, of the reminiscences of childhood which occupied his[208] mind almost exclusively at the end, & which he transmitted[209] to the sympathetic monk. This one was fully conversant with the house in the Karlstrasse, with my grandmother's careful huswif[e]ry, the boyish games & harmless occupations of Papa & his brothers, the fruit-trees in their little garden, the cobbled yard with the nasturtiums, vines, & the neighbour's nut-tree hanging over the low wall.

---

[206] The final sentence of this paragraph, beginning with 'And as a last resort' added by hand in the lower margin of the page.
[207] Hewitt typed 'wish or desire', but crossed out the first two words.
[208] 'my father's' crossed out and 'his' typed above the line.
[209] '(recounted)' struck through.

Living it all over again, so tenderly,[210] & lingering over every detail in the leisure of a gentle death, my father became truly[211] as a little child. His last word, when he had seemed unconscious for hours, was "*Bad!*" (Engl. Bath), coming strangely at the appointed time for this function. It summed up two of his characteristics, his[212] punctuality & love of cleanliness. But the Brother shook his head; they could not bath him now, for he was much too weak. And so he slept instead & did not wake any more.[213]

From the general account given here of my father you might possibly imagine that he was as easy to deal with as a child. But are children so easy to deal with? [A]re they not unaccountable quantities? And that was what he was, – with all his simplicity & naiveté – utterly unaccountable. Now dense & now pretending to be dense; at one time amused & at another time irritated by the same cause. Perhaps he was more dependent on the state of his health than most people, & had less self-control. [p. 370] Such control as he had was from habit, & from a more or less lonely life that had of necessity taught him to be self-contained.

The sketch or portrait – I hardly know what to call it – which I have attempted, is, at least as far as memory permits, an accurate & exhaustive one. I trust it attains a little more than the surface correctness of a photographer who has failed to catch the spirit.

HHHHHHHHHHHHHHHHHHHHHHHHHHHHHHHHH
XXXXXXXXXXXXXXXXXXXXXXXXXXXXXXXXXX
HHHHHHHHHHHHHHHHHHHHHHHHHHHHHHHHHH

---

[210] 'in every detail' crossed out.

[211] 'once more' crossed out.

[212] '(love of)' struck through.

[213] Hewitt here inserts a few brief items written or collected by her father, which have been excluded from the edition due to their lack of contextual coherence. As she herself notes: "I offer it [this snippet] without context".

Correspondence regarding publication

The letters are held at the Taylor Institution Library, shelfmark MS. 8° E.43.

Benjamin Ifor Evans to Luisa Hewitt

26.1.32

Dear Madam,

I return the MSS. separately. I have read them & enjoyed them. I did not know when you returned from Germany, or I would have sent them off sooner. They go to-night, or tomorrow, by registered post, under separate cover. I wonder if you meant me to add comment. I am not good at giving practical comments on work, but, in case you wished me to do so, I have noted down a few points, which we could discuss when we meet. I say nothing of the verse. I have never written verses that I thought well of, & if one can't do this one's comments are not likely to be useful. Also you have Rollo[1] at hand. I think if you publish the sonnets ever I should forget Pinto: he is rather out of place there.

The form is very interesting. Frankly I think you have the material for a book there, but not yet the book itself. You do not decide clearly what you want to do, and this, as I will try & show brings in irrelevant material. Further you do not decide between the details which reveal & the details which are interesting only to yourself. Look if you will at the chapter where the Gounod incident is told. That "nymph" is excellently described & the whole of the matter well-handled. But it is strangled by idle reminiscences of other mistresses of the school variety etc. who do not matter a damn. Is it not possibl[e] to rebuild such a chapter concentrating on the three or four people who matter & with Sister Agatha shown more fully?

---

[1] 'Rollo' was the nickname of Reginald Mainwaring Hewitt, as evidenced by letters preserved in his archive at the University of Nottingham.

This again comes through in your treatment of "The father". Some of this is admirably done (e.g. p. 13) but it gets into discursiveness. I know that, Gibbon-like, you want to tell the truth. But then why not follow Gibbon & not Gibbon's precepts. He obviously selects, arranges & works-up. I think that there must be more of this working up. For instance I should bring all of "the father" material into the early chapters. It would strengthen the early part.

I think too that you do not bring out visual elements enough. Do you ever describe your father or your mother? This I find missing in the school-day scenes. I miss it in your poetry too. It doesn't matter there, but I do not see how you can manage without it here.

Then on this matter of detail again. Take the scene of your mother's death. It seems to me that the egg incident, useful as it is[,] runs away with the balance of incident there. The difficulty is I think to extract from mere memory what is imaginatively convincing.

I dare say you will disagree with much of this & possibly you will be right. I may have missed your purpose but I do feel that more clarity could be gained by more attention to form, which you seem at turns consciously to avoid.

The style varies. I find it heavy at first, & in the *Foreword* (sometimes later) ungrammatical. This is probably the typist. It is strong & beautiful frequently especially some of the father scenes.

I enjoyed it: there is a book in it: but I think you have got to get to work again to get that book out of it. Now curse me if you will!

The English Association wants Rollo in the Autumn, so we shall have our party then if not before. It's been a rotten term. We get a cut of salaries in April. I hope you fare better.

I love you both, B. I.

P.S. I have re-read this & decided that I have not brought out how much I liked it. But enlarging on that will not help you. The only criticism I have ever found useful is the type of friendly carping which I have indulged in. I hope we know each other well enough to do it.

Luisa Hewitt to John Simon Gabriel Simmons

Nottingham, Sept. 5th.

Dear Mr. Simmons

Replies to your requests are all in the affirmative: Yes... yes... Certainly. But I have been on the daily more blunted point of writing to you *my* apologies for sending the chapter unrevised, & as far as I recollect full of camouflageries! I cannot bear to re-read anything written so long ago. Prof. B. I. Evans thought this m.s. had the *makings* of a good book, which at once put it out of count for me, as I never re-write anything, I prefer to start on something new. Basil Blackwell, a friend, & the only publisher on whom I inflicted it, said that readers don't like to have to 'chew their wine', that in fact the book was too long-winded to be 'suitable for publication'. So you see 'influence' doesn't always help. Of course I should have liked & still would like to see this bit of autobiography in print; but not at the cost of having to pull it together, though I might cut out some passages & do away with the silly camouflage, which after all these years is quite superfluous. Prof. Evans refused to believe that every word is gospel truth – its only recommendation if it *is* one. Fact is always stranger if less artistic than Fiction. Once I sent some plays to Lilian Bayliss for criticism, & of the only one which was pure fact she wrote that it was impossible & that the characters would never have behaved as in reality they did! I am at present engaged on a diary of much later date in which fact & fiction are blended, at least I sometimes throw two characters into one, which amuses me, though whether it makes them convincing is another question.

Yours sincerely,
Luisa Hewitt

P.S. As my husband – the critic par excellence – once said, there is no point, unless possibly from the psychiatrist's angle, of recording simply every detail one *chances* to remember: one must select the important from so much that is necessarily accidental. That is what I find so difficult to do.

[Handwritten postscript:] I will post the m.s. to-morrow.

John Simon Gabriel Simmons to Luisa Hewitt

7 October 1952

Dear Mrs Hewett [sic],

My letters always begin with an apology, I fear. And for the best of reasons, since I can never write as soon as I intend. I am so sorry to have been so long in writing about the MS., but it took time to read, and the time took some finding.

I found it intensely interesting, but agree with your critic that it needs tautening if it is to be published. The Father Chapter, by the way, struck me as being by far the best part of the whole, but even that would need polishing, I think, to make it fully effective. So unless you are prepared to give time to it I don't imagine that publication would be possible. I am seeing a 'successful novelist' this evening and will try to find out in general terms how one could best set about it, granted a MS. which was bright and shining and fit for the press.

Meanwhile, as regards the actual text: I take it that you would not object to my having a copy typed of (a) the first dozen pages (which set the scene in the Taylorian), and (b) of the Father Chapter. I would like to keep one copy myself, and deposit others in the Taylorian and Bodleian Libraries. It would be for you to decide under what conditions these shd be deposited, e.g. that they might be freely consulted, but not quoted from during your life-time without your permission. Or, of course, unconditionally. I don't myself see that any harm could come to anybody in the unlikely event of quotation being made in the near future. But the historian of the Taylorian writing to celebrate its bi-centenary in 2044 would be very pleased to enliven his story from your *Selbstzeugnis*!

I cannot easily arrange for the entire MS. to be re-typed for the Bodleian, so since you do not wish to place your single copy there immediately, may I in a macabre way suggest that you think of putting a little note on it which would bring it to the Bodleian eventually – that is, if you 'agree in principle', as I gathered from your letter you do?

One further point. I have managed to disentangle most of your concealed names, but I am uncertain or ignorant of the true equivalents of those I have listed. Could you put names to them for me? I know that this will sound pettifogging, but our future historian will bless you for the keys. I know to my cost how difficult it is to penetrate pseudonyms after a century or so.

Your letter to me opened with the words 'yes, yes, yes'. But I have no copy of the questions I asked you. I hope that I haven't taken your agreement too much for granted in what I have written above. If I have, do please tell me.

I'm sorry to be so unencouraging about publication, and hope that this hasn't quite veiled my expression of the interest [*The letter breaks off here; the remainder of the page is lost*].

HHHHHHHHHHHHHHHHHHHHHHHHHHHHHHHH
XXXXXXXXXXXXXXXXXXXXXXXXXXXXXXXX
HHHHHHHHHHHHHHHHHHHHHHHHHHHHHHHH

Plans of the Taylor Institution Library

In 1932, an extension to the library was built. The new part of the building includes a floor between the ground floor and the first floor of the old building. In the older part of the building, which is relevant to this edition, a staircase leads directly from the ground floor to what is now the second floor. The old floorplans can be consulted in *Plans of the extension to the building by architect T Harold Hughes. 1931*, Oxford, Bodleian Libraries, University Archives, TL 5/17/2–4.

The plans below are based on the <u>modern plans available online</u> as part of the modern library guide. The labels, based on Luisa Hewitt's description, were provided by Emma Huber and Christina Ostermann.

Historic postcard of the Taylor Institution Library[1]

---

[1] I thank David Hambleton and Emma Huber for bringing this postcard to my attention and providing a scan.

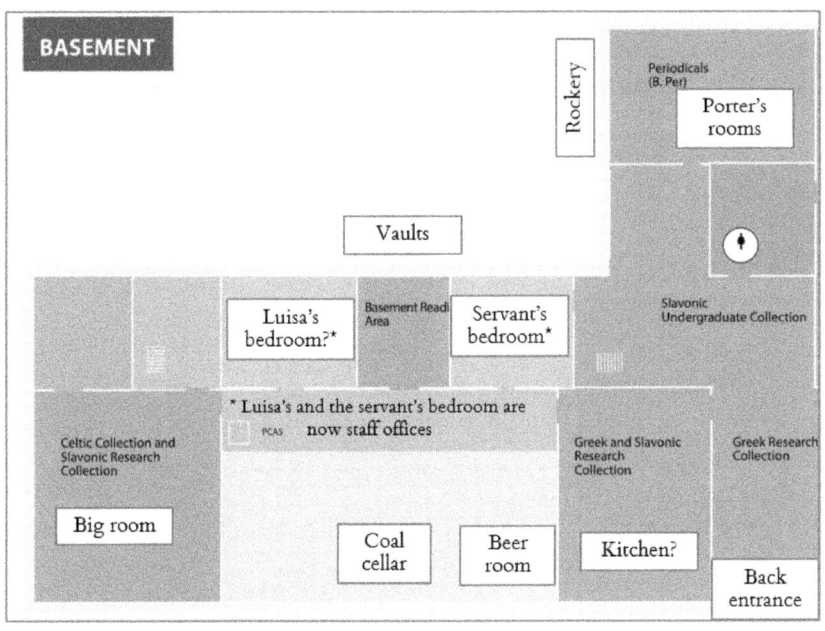

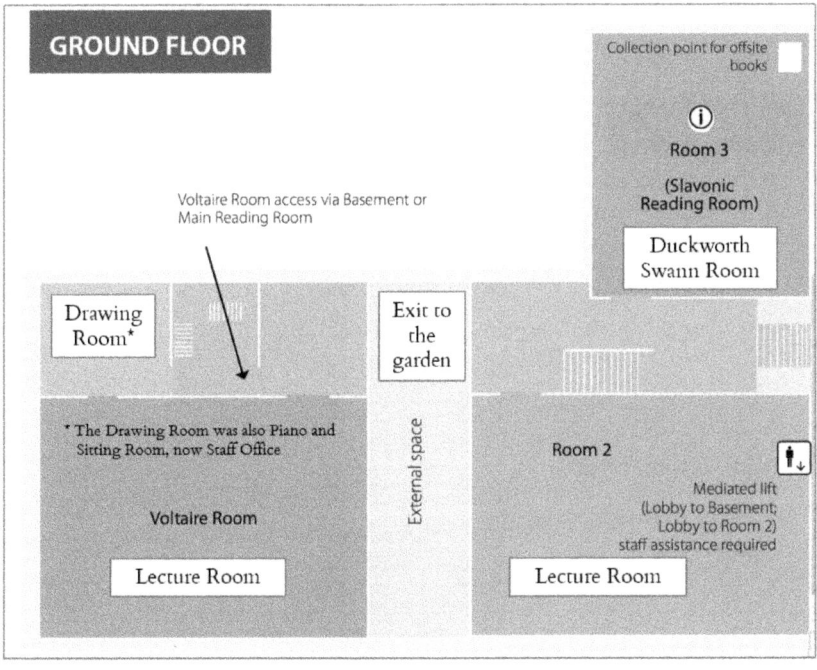

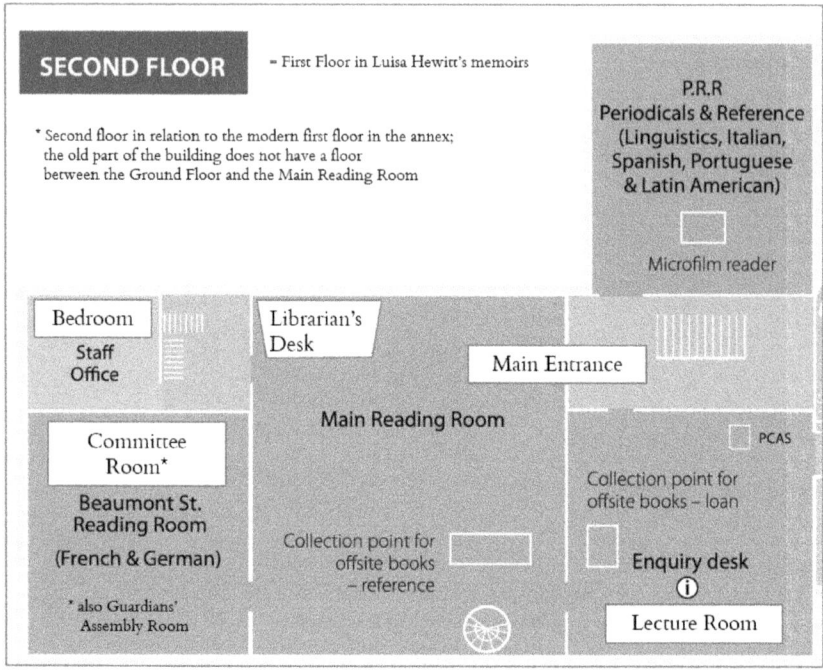

First Floor

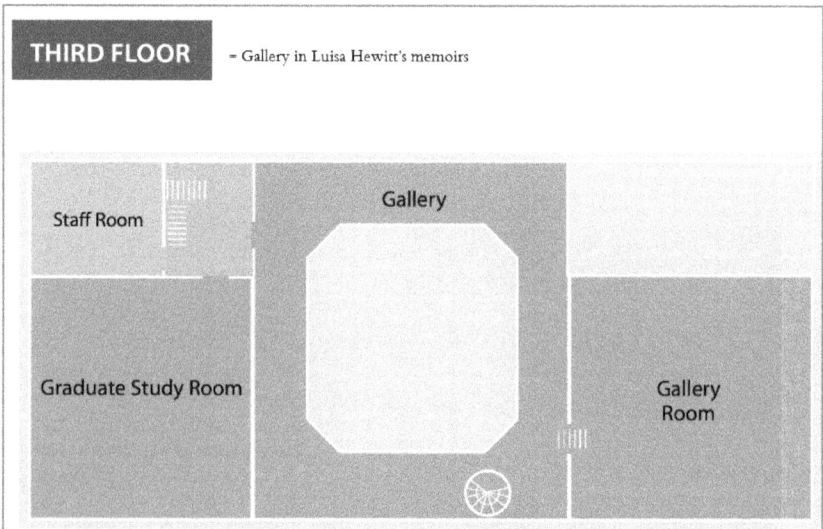

Gallery Level